W9-BNV-201

To Dad

From

_____

On this date

_____

# PRAYERS & PROMISES
## *for* DADS

JOHN HUDSON TINER

BARBOUR
PUBLISHING

© 2005 by Barbour Publishing

ISBN 1-59310-646-7

All rights reserved. No part of this publication may be reproduced or transmitted for commercial purposes, except for brief quotations in printed reviews, without written permission of the publisher.

Churches and other noncommercial interests may reproduce portions of this book without the express written permission of Barbour Publishing, provided that the text does not exceed 500 words or 5 percent of the entire book, whichever is less, and that the text is not material quoted from another publisher. When reproducing text from this book, include the following credit line: "From *Prayers & Promises for Dads*, published by Barbour Publishing, Inc. Used by permission."

Scripture quotations marked KJV are taken from the King James Version of the Bible.

Scripture quotations marked NRSV are taken from the New Revised Standard Version Bible, copyright 1989, Division of Christian Education of the National Council of the Churches of Christ in the United States of America. Used by permission. All rights reserved.

Scripture quotations marked NIV are taken from the HOLY BIBLE, NEW INTERNATIONAL VERSION®. NIV®. Copyright © 1973, 1978, 1984 by International Bible Society. Used by permission of Zondervan. All rights reserved.

Cover image © Steve Gardner, Pixelworks Studio

Published by Barbour Publishing, Inc., P.O. Box 719, Uhrichsville, Ohio 44683
www.barbourbooks.com

*Our mission is to publish and distribute inspirational products offering exceptional value and biblical encouragement to the masses.*

ecpa Member of the
Evangelical Christian
Publishers Association

Printed in China.
5 4 3 2 1

To Adam, Sydney, Samuel, Matthew, Megan, and Christian

# Contents

# PREFACE

The thought-provoking prayers on these pages are written especially for dads, from a dad's perspective. The prayers appeal to the emotion as well as the intellect and draw the heart and mind closer to God by expressing thanksgiving, happiness, patience, and obedience.

All prayers begin with a scripture quotation. The verses are compelling reminders that God promises to bless dads who speak to Him with humility and live faithfully. As the Bible directs, "Listen, children, to a father's instruction, and be attentive, that you may gain insight; for I give you good precepts: do not forsake my teaching" (Proverbs 4:1–2 NRSV).

# TARGET

*With this in mind, we constantly pray for you, that our God may count you worthy of his calling, and that by his power he may fulfill every good purpose of yours and every act prompted by your faith.*

2 THESSALONIANS 1:11 NIV

Father, I've seen people who have chosen a goal for their life's work when they were young and reached their target as straight as an arrow shot by a skilled archer. I've seen others follow a long and tortuous path to their eventual goal. Sometimes parents who try to live their children's lives for them have caused the deviation.

Lord, it is a fine line that I must follow in helping my children decide upon a career. Give me the parenting skill to direct rather than suppress the aspirations of my children. You have plans for them. Help me overcome excessive caution that may influence them to miss the opportunities that You are opening for them.

Father, I pray that we will search Your Word, pray, and listen to Your voice to learn what You have in mind for us. Help us be flexible enough to allow Your hands to mold us.

# GOALS

*And that ye study to be quiet, and to do your own business,*
*and to work with your own hands, as we commanded you;*
*That ye may walk honestly toward them that are without,*
*and that ye may have lack of nothing.*

1 THESSALONIANS 4:11–12 KJV

Father, I need to have aspirations. Left without goals, I would only feed my desire for pleasure. Help me gain an understanding of Your will for me. Give me insight and guide me to problems worthy of attack.

Lord, sometimes the clutter of my life blocks my aspirations. At other times, I am too easily persuaded that my goals cannot be reached or that an easier way will lead to success. Help me be an example to my children of a purpose-driven life.

Father, I want to have a life in which I strive to meet my goals. But I pray that I do not become so overwhelmed with my aspirations that I betray my Christian disposition. I've seen people who undertake an important task and become obsessed with success. They become belligerent with anyone who doesn't share their vision. They exercise brutal force over anyone who dares to disagree with them. As I press ahead, help me remain cheerful, even-tempered, and polite.

# GROWTH

*Let us therefore follow after the things which make for peace,*
*and things wherewith one may edify another.*

ROMANS 14:19 KJV

Father, I realize that some goals cannot be achieved, but they are worth the effort anyway. By accepting the challenge, I grow and gain abilities that I would not develop otherwise. I do not know in my own life where difficulty ends and the impossible begins. But I pray that I'll continue to strive for excellence even when the prospects are against me.

Lord, I pray that my children will pursue their dreams, too. Help us aim high. Even if we do not succeed, help us grow because of the attempt. Please help us live lives that make a difference.

Father, guide me to recognize the fact that the Bible addresses all of my hopes and fears. It guides me to the goals to which I should aspire. May I help my children see that their lives will be richer by following the course that brings them closer to Your perfection.

# ACHIEVEMENT

*Therefore prepare your minds for action; discipline yourselves;*
*set all your hope on the grace that Jesus Christ*
*will bring you when he is revealed.*

1 PETER 1:13 NRSV

Father, I want to be an achiever, although I do not always understand where my real talents lie. I often begin projects but let my enthusiasm for them grow cold when I see that I am unlikely to develop a superior ability at them. I realize, too late, that I have invested time and effort into a project that did not have Your blessing.

Lord, help me grasp the fact that my greatest efforts should be directed toward how I lead my life as a Christian. Please guide me to goals that are worthy of my efforts—goals that will bring satisfaction because I am doing them for You.

Father, remind me that my aspirations should not be for skill at an established occupation or success in a specific undertaking. Instead, my aim should be to prepare myself to be a good leader of my family and for whatever other jobs You have in mind for me.

# TIME

*I have shown you all things, how that so labouring ye ought to support the weak, and to remember the words of the Lord Jesus, how he said, It is more blessed to give than to receive.*

ACTS 20:35 KJV

Father, upon my return from a business trip, my young children asked me to play, and it took a determined effort to do so because I had spent all of my energy at work. I realize that if I do not play with my little ones while I have them, they will soon spring up, and then the opportunity will be lost. I can constantly pursue my business only at the neglect of many other things, including my family.

Lord, help me recognize the importance of devoting a special portion of my time to play with my children. They need quality time, but unless I provide the quantity, I will not be there when the special need arises.

Father, when my children were learning to walk, I would hold them to keep them from falling. Now they are older, but they still need my time and support to assure their success at other endeavors. Help me prepare them for the future.

## PRESENCE IN MIND

*"Now my eyes will be open and my ears attentive*
*to the prayer that is made in this place.*
*For now I have chosen and consecrated this house*
*so that my name may be there forever;*
*my eyes and my heart will be there for all time."*

2 CHRONICLES 7:15–16 NRSV

Lord, when I am with my children, I am always conscious that I am a father. My actions more readily conform to what I should do and say. I am kinder, more affectionate, and ever helpful. I take seriously my duty to guide, discipline, and teach how they should conduct themselves. Help me realize that even when they are not in my presence, my duties as a father do not cease. As the head of my family, I represent them to the community. I am paving the way for them.

Father, I pray, too, that I will influence my children for good even when they are not in my presence. Help them see my smile, listen to my words, and follow my guidance. I pray that my influence persists even when I am physically absent. Dear Father, help me also be mindful of Your presence in my life.

# PRESENCE

*And he said, My presence shall go with thee,*
*and I will give thee rest.*

EXODUS 33:14 KJV

Father, I know that a situation becomes worse when the mind is troubled. But support and encouragement can overcome bleak times. Sometimes my role as father is merely to be there.

While my daughter was doing volunteer work at the hospital, she was accused of taking a piece of jewelry. When I arrived and stood at her side, my presence gave her confidence. With cool and convincing words, she stated her innocence. I am thankful that a short time later a relative of the patient notified the hospital that the item had been found where it had been placed for safekeeping.

To my daughter, it was not the number of people who stood by her side, but her confidence in the one who did. Heavenly Father, how great You are because You stand by me despite my shortcomings. I know Your presence upholds me in the face of strong opposition. Help me emulate You in being there for my family.

## NEVER RESIGN

*"O LORD, God of our fathers Abraham, Isaac and Israel. . .*
*give my son Solomon the wholehearted devotion*
*to keep your commands, requirements and decrees."*

1 CHRONICLES 29:18–19 NIV

Father, my children are entering their teenage years when the choices they make can have impacts far greater than when they were younger. At this stage in their lives, there are many hazardous attitudes that I could take. I could become over-bearing with a "Follow the rules, or else!" attitude. Or, at any hint of problem, I could overreact quickly, without thinking. I may incorrectly believe it is impossible for them to do wrong because I've trained them so well. I've also seen fathers who resign as parents at this stage because they no longer think they can make a difference.

Lord, help me realize that I can make a difference. I must not abdicate my responsibilities as a father merely because the task has become more difficult. Help me guide my teenagers to accurately per-ceive the right choices and the true way based on Your Word.

# ACCEPTANCE

*May the God of hope fill you with all joy and peace in believing,
so that you may abound in hope by the power of the Holy Spirit.*

ROMANS 15:13 NRSV

Father, when I was a little child, I visited my grandmother who had this soft, down-filled feather bed. On a chilly morning, I would sink into it and be toasty warm. Grandma called it a comforter. I thought the name fit exactly because it gave me a pleasant, secure feeling.

Lord, I can still use a spiritual comforter. It usually happens when the chill of self-doubt attacks me. I give up on myself. I think I'll never learn how to successfully complete an assignment, or that when it is complete, a glaring error will be visible. I fear that those who depend on me will turn away in disappointment.

Lord, I often see this same insecurity in my children. I am astonished at how critical they can be of themselves. I realize now the importance of the comfort of Your Holy Spirit. Help us all remember that You accept us regardless of our shortcomings.

# CONNECTION

*Am I now trying to win the approval of men, or of God?*
*Or am I trying to please men?*
*If I were still trying to please men,*
*I would not be a servant of Christ.*

GALATIANS 1:10 NIV

Father, at one time I did not fully commit myself to You. I sought to associate with others whom I imagined would fill my need to belong. I scheduled group activities, joined clubs, and found hobbies I could share with others. Yet these did not bring the sense of belonging that I sought. Even with the swirl of activity around me, I felt empty and isolated. The connection to others only became satisfying after I first connected to You.

Lord, I've seen young people who think glitz, frantic activities, and mindless pursuits will fill a void in their lives. I can understand their desperate search because I have felt it, too. But I no longer have an incessant worry about belonging because I belong to You, and that is enough. I pray that I have shown my children that a better life comes simply from being close to You.

# SUPPORT

*"Take my yoke upon you, and learn from me;*
*for I am gentle and humble in heart,*
*and you will find rest for your souls.*
*For my yoke is easy, and my burden is light."*

MATTHEW 11:29−30 NRSV

Father, an outdoor magazine recommended using a hiking stick to make hiking easier. The extra support would prevent falling when negotiating a difficult, rock-strewn trail. But I refused to accept that the aid of a hiking stick would benefit me. In my stubbornness, I decided to ignore the advice and avoid the extra bother of carrying a stick. I wanted to do it myself and be self-reliant.

Lord, I often fall into the deception of thinking that I do not need anything to lean on in my spiritual life. But my traverse of this life is filled with difficulties far more dangerous than an uneven trail. Help me put aside the misconception that I need no one but myself. Help me develop the humility to recognize that I need to lean on You.

Father, I pray that neither my family nor I ever stand so sure of ourselves that we think we can never stumble. May we always be willing to seek Your comfort and support.

# REFUGE

*God is our refuge and strength, an ever-present help in trouble.*
*Therefore we will not fear, though the earth give way*
*and the mountains fall into the heart of the sea.*

PSALM 46:1–2 NIV

Father, I've read that some animals in Africa become frightened at the sound of the lion's powerful roar. Often they are in a brush pile where they have perfect safety. But they bolt from their cover, and in their confusion they run toward the lion rather than away from it.

Lord, the evil desires in my life—anger, envy, covetousness, and addictions—are constantly trying to pull me from my place of safety with You. I must keep You clearly in mind as my place of refuge. Otherwise, when dangerous desires call me, I might run the wrong way. It is not enough to merely rid my life of these wicked attractions. I must anchor my heart in Your love.

Father, I pray that my children will learn the importance of knowing that You are their shelter. By reading the Bible, praying, developing Christian friendships, and obeying You, they will have protection from the world's evil intentions.

# EQUIPPED

*May the God of peace. . .equip you with everything good*
*for doing his will, and may he work in us what is pleasing to him,*
*through Jesus Christ, to whom be glory for ever and ever. Amen.*

HEBREWS 13:20–21 NIV

Father, as I grew up, my father experienced terrible economic conditions. Every day was a financial struggle, and he did not have the advantage of a network of supportive family members. At times, it must have been a severe temptation to give up. But he embraced You rather than the world. He never abdicated his duties as a father.

Heavenly Father, I've seen supervisors in the place where I work be promoted to positions for which they are ill suited. They have the luxury of delegating those tasks in which they are incompetent to others. But a good father cannot give away his duties or decide that he no longer wants to be a father. He must continue.

Lord, bless me so I will have the patience and dedication to be a first-rate father. Open my eyes to Your Word so I see those scriptures that will equip me for my responsibilities in raising my children.

# GENUINE

*Hide your face from my sins and blot out all my iniquity.*
*Create in me a pure heart,*
*O God, and renew a steadfast spirit within me.*

PSALM 51:9–10 NIV

Father, when my children are sorry for some infraction of the rules, I explain that the proof of their repentance is their commitment to do better. It is not in their outward show, which can be a sham, but in whether they make a sincere effort to improve.

Lord, sometimes I find myself less than authentic when I feign commitment to a worthy cause. I nod wisely, readily agree that something needs to be done, and then walk away and forget the matter entirely. Please forgive me, and strengthen me so that my heart is without deceit.

Father, when I make a commitment, help me stand behind it because it has my full and honest endorsement. May I feel bound to bring the task to successful completion. Strengthen my resolve to be an example to my children of the importance of making a genuine effort to fulfill commitments.

# PRIMARY DUTY

*That he would grant unto us, that we being delivered*
*out of the hand of our enemies might serve him without fear,*
*In holiness and righteousness before him, all the days of our life.*

LUKE 1:74–75 KJV

Father, my company requires me to investigate injuries on the job, determine the cause, and propose how to prevent the accident from happening again. In many cases, I've found that accidents occur when a person tries to accomplish two tasks at the same time. Neither one is done well. The balancing act of trying to satisfy two different goals leads to disaster. Accident victims often do not have a clear commitment to their primary task, and they become indecisive when they must choose between their main duty and a secondary function.

In Your Word, Lord, I read about the impossibility of serving two masters. I commit to You my time, talent, money, and my physical and emotional energy. I pray that I will be single-minded so that when a situation calls for action I will not hesitate to serve You. I pray that my children will recognize that decisions become easier once they develop the clear purpose to serve You first.

# SELF-HELP

*For, "All men are like grass, and all their glory is like the flowers of
the field; the grass withers and the flowers fall, but the word of the
Lord stands forever." And this is the word that was preached to you.*

1 PETER 1:24–25 NIV

Lord, around the office, I see people carrying self-help
books to read during their lunch break. Another title makes
the best-seller list each month. Yet few of these books
have enough substance to be enduring classics.

Heavenly Father, when I think about the makeup of my personality, I find many constants—I am sinful, selfish, full of pride,
and sometimes afraid. My greatest concerns are the inadequacies that
I find in my character, especially those of being a family leader. And
so, I am committed to taking the steps that will bring me closer to
being a good father.

Lord, the Bible addresses all these issues that I face. Your Word
is more thorough than any contemporary book that tries to show me
how to improve myself. May I always remember to turn to Your
enduring guidebook for daily living and
eternal salvation.

# MEANINGFUL

*Do not let any unwholesome talk come out of your mouths,*
*but only what is helpful for building others up according to their needs,*
*that it may benefit those who listen.*

EPHESIANS 4:29 NIV

Lord, I have seen relationships between husband and wife and between father and children dissolve because of a failure to communicate. The lack of an interchange of thoughts and information caused erosion in the family camaraderie. I ask that You will help me to relate well with my wife and children. May my conversation with them be more than mere words. Help me express myself in a way that is readily and clearly understood. Help me listen in such a way that I hear not only the words of my children but also the ideas and heartfelt concerns that they convey.

On a spiritual level, I pray that my heavenly communication keeps an open line. Help me to continually evaluate my relationship with You. Staying in contact with You, Lord, has eternal importance to help me realize my blessings and translate them into actions to share with others.

# POWER

*In this way the word of the Lord spread widely and grew in power.*

ACTS 19:20 NIV

Father, I read well-known Bible stories such as the miracle of loaves and fishes to my little children. I am amazed at how the stories capture their minds. Sometimes they ask me to read the same story over and over until they have it memorized.

Lord, for my own study, I am reading the book of Acts. Throughout it I find stories that range from Paul's emotional farewell at Ephesus to the exciting adventure of his shipwreck on the way to Rome.

Father, I am constantly amazed at the power of the Bible to touch the lives of people regardless of their age, education, or economic level. Long ago, shepherds and others with humble backgrounds first heard the simple parables spoken by Your Son. Today, the lives of well-educated city dwellers are being touched by the same parables. Father, may I continue to open my heart to the power of the Bible.

# DAILY

*Rejoice always, pray without ceasing, give thanks in all circumstances; for this is the will of God in Christ Jesus for you.*

1 THESSALONIANS 5:16—18 NRSV

Father, I have come into my room alone to spend some time with You. I am dismayed when I realize how much time has passed since we have talked without interruptions. I know I have spoken with You throughout the day, and that in doing so I had Your undivided attention. But my mind has been flooded with distractions, so my attentiveness wavers.

Lord, should my children come to me to discuss subjects of importance, I give them my full attention, and I expect them to do the same. Yet I often fail to allot uninterrupted time for prayer. Please forgive me.

Father, when I face a stressful interview at work, I rehearse in my mind what I am going to say. I polish the sentences until they express precisely what I mean. I am thankful, Lord, that I can come to You without rehearsal. Regardless of how poorly I express myself, You know the concerns that are on my mind. Help me to bring them to You every day.

# REQUESTS

*Be careful for nothing; but in every thing by prayer and supplication
with thanksgiving let your requests be made known unto God.
And the peace of God, which passeth all understanding,
shall keep your hearts and minds through Christ Jesus.*

PHILIPPIANS 4:6−7 KJV

Father, I am aware of many people who are suffering and in difficult situations. I pray that they and their families will be able to work out the difficulties. Help me to find a way to help ease their burdens.

Father, sometimes my own children have problems, but because of their lack of experience, they cannot express what is troubling them. Their distress can go unnoticed unless I devote time to being with them and talking with them. Guide me to giving them the support they need. Help them realize that they can make their requests known to me—and to You.

# GENEROSITY

*"Give, and it will be given to you. A good measure, pressed down,*
*shaken together and running over, will be poured into your lap.*
*For with the measure you use, it will be measured to you."*

LUKE 6:38 NIV

L ord, You set the standard for generosity by giving Your life
for a sinful world. May I always be reminded of Your sacrifice when I see a need that I can serve. Just like a farmer
who plants seeds and profits from a harvest, You also bless those who
share their assets.

Lord, to show kindness, one must be thoughtful. One of my
son's friends had agreed to do extra chores for his family. But when
the friend became injured, my son volunteered to do the chores until
his friend recovered. I appreciate the fact that my son
thought beyond himself. Father, please help me
continue to encourage him to think about others so
his character will become even more generous.

Heavenly Father, also help me to give with
a pure motive to bless those in need and
not for the selfish reason that I expect
to be rewarded. I truly want to be Your
hand extended to help those who have
physical, spiritual, and financial needs.

# RESCUE

*Inasmuch as ye have done it unto one of the least of these my brethren,*
*ye have done it unto me.*

MATTHEW 25:40 KJV

Lord Jesus, I read in the Bible that when I come to the rescue of those who are hungry and thirsty, I am loving You. Help me never accept pain and suffering as a natural condition. Guide me to show the compassion that You had when You healed the sick and fed the hungry multitudes. Give me the ability to put sympathy into action for those who suffer.

Lord, help me overcome the thought that someone—whether acquaintance or stranger—is unworthy of compassion. May Your rich blessings fall upon my family and me so that we can be contributors of aid rather than recipients.

Heavenly Father, I thank You for Your continual watchful eye upon me. Guide me to bring a concrete expression of love to others who have a physical or emotional crisis. Provide me with the wisdom to relieve the suffering of others.

# MERCY

*Be kind to one another, tenderhearted, forgiving one another,*
*as God in Christ has forgiven you.*

EPHESIANS 4:32 NRSV

Father, not only does compassion restore order to shattered lives, it brings people back from the brink of hopelessness. It is a catalyst that starts them on the road to recovery. Help me develop awareness of the distress of others and strengthen my determination to relieve it.

Lord, sometimes the fact that an acquaintance needs compassion creeps up on me—an aged neighbor, a relative who has become sick, a friend who is struggling with a chronic illness, a former coworker who has been unemployed. Help me recognize and respond to these very evident needs.

Father, I desire to be a more compassionate person. Help me be kind and forgiving. Give me a heart full of mercy. Help me identify those ways in which I can serve others. Guide me to enlist the assistance of my family so they learn how to serve You by helping others.

# STRANGERS

*"Love your enemies, do good to those who hate you,*
*bless those who curse you, pray for those who abuse you.*
*Do to others as you would have them do to you."*

LUKE 6:27–28, 31 NRSV

Father, I know that compassion for others begins with an awareness of their suffering, followed by a desire to relieve it. But compassion is not complete until I take action. It is easy to follow my heart into action for close family members and for others who are important to me, but it is more difficult to help strangers.

Lord, I confess that even when I develop an impulse to help, I am reluctant to involve myself with those I do not know. Many needy individuals suffer situations so severe that I have difficulty even imagining what they must endure. I despair that my efforts would not have a lasting benefit.

Father, help me see people around me through Your caring eyes. Although I may not have the special skills to meet every need, give me the determination not to be afraid to be kind. Let me show mercy so that mercy will be mine when I come to You.

# INVESTMENT

*And those who know your name put their trust in you, for you,*
*O LORD, have not forsaken those who seek you.*

PSALM 9:10 NRSV

Father, each morning I read the business section of the newspaper. The economic future looks bright one day, but the next day projections are bleak. I carefully invest my meager resources, but the fluctuation of interest rates and an unstable stock market make me wary. None of the choices are completely free of risk. Things can go drastically wrong in a heartbeat.

Lord, I am unable to see what the future holds, but I trust You as the One who holds the future. Life's wealth often comes and goes, but my security is in You, my Provider.

Father, as my children grow and develop, their needs rapidly change. Provide me with the skills and resources I need to promote their continued growth. I invest my trust in You to guide me to meet the physical, emotional, and spiritual needs of my family. Help me make my first and most important investment in my family.

# IN GOD

*May the God of hope fill you with all joy and peace as you trust in him,
so that you may overflow with hope by the power of the Holy Spirit.*

ROMANS 15:13 NIV

Father, having confidence is easy when I am not under attack. It is only when I am belittled or ridiculed that my confidence can crumble. My wife and children love and respect me, and my friends encourage me, but the greatest security comes from trusting You.

Lord, I must not think that having wealth or power will give me confidence. Help me develop the calm confidence that comes from upholding righteous convictions. May my children see my example so they understand that confidence is void unless it is exercised for good.

Father, may I be faithful in putting my trust in You. May my prayers for strength to overcome difficulties always come from an honest heart. Protect me from wavering as I follow You.

# TRUST

*Trust in the LORD with all thine heart;*
*and lean not unto thine own understanding.*
*In all thy ways acknowledge him, and he shall direct thy paths.*

PROVERBS 3:5–6 KJV

Father, when I first came to You, I was so determined to do great works that I considered little jobs beneath my effort. When I fell short of my goals, I despaired of ever doing anything for You. All along, a multitude of small deeds had been available, but I ignored them.

Father, I am careful to give my children tasks within their ability. For a more difficult assignment, I help them move toward the final goal in easy stages. Should a problem arise, I am willing to step in and help them. They have no reason to be apprehensive that they might fail. Soon they can do the entire task on their own.

Lord, I realize now that in the little tasks You are preparing me for a larger mission. Grant me the eyes to see little jobs that need to be done and the willing heart to do them.

# HUMILITY

*All of you must clothe yourselves with humility*
*in your dealings with one another, for*
*"God opposes the proud, but gives grace to the humble."*

1 PETER 5:5 NRSV

ather, sometimes I feel so uncertain of myself that I cannot achieve my goals because the slightest criticism or hint that I may be on the wrong path paralyzes me into inaction. At other times, I develop self-confidence but only generate it by thinking more highly of myself than I ought. In between the two extremes, I wish to develop calm confidence without the haughty attitude that befalls those who think they are always right.

Lord, may nothing in my manner suggest arrogance. Any success that I reap is because You planted the seed. I want to base my self-confidence not upon myself, but on the One I walk beside. My confidence is built when I welcome You into my heart and mind and lay myself bare before You.

Father, my trust is not in myself, but in You. Help me to lead my family with confidence.

# JOURNEY

*I have learned the secret of being content in any and every situation,*
*whether well fed or hungry, whether living in plenty or in want.*
*I can do everything through him who gives me strength.*

PHILIPPIANS 4:12—13 NIV

Dear Lord, when I was a child, my father drove along a road where a rainbow seemed to end just over the next hill. But no matter how far we traveled, we never reached the end of the rainbow. It was always ahead of us.

Father, as an adult I have set many goals that I thought would bring contentment if I could only achieve them. But I discovered that no matter what I achieved, contentment stayed out of reach. Thank You for showing me that contentment is not a destination but the way I make my journey.

Lord, help me set worthy goals and encourage my children to do the same. But also guide us to set goals based on what You want us to do rather than what we imagine will bring pleasure, success, and contentment. Instead of looking forward in discontent for better situations, let us focus on what You have given us. May we see our cup as running over with Your blessings.

# PRESTIGE

*But godliness with contentment is great gain.*
*For we brought nothing into this world,*
*and it is certain we can carry nothing out.*
*And having food and raiment let us be therewith content.*

1 TIMOTHY 6:6−8 KJV

Heavenly Father, as a teenager, I dreamed of owning a big, four-wheel-drive pickup truck. I imagined how it would impress the girl who took my order in the drive-through at the fast-food restaurant. Today, I smile at those juvenile attempts to get the attention of someone whose name I can no longer remember.

Father, I pray that my children will develop good judgment of what is important. But I must continually remind myself to do so, too, because I still find myself trying to impress people. I sometimes engage in silly, immature behavior as I chase empty prestige and status. I still fall into the trap of trying to impress people by my possessions.

Lord, I humbly pray that I will be content with the blessings You give. Help me focus my thoughts on living a dedicated life. Remind me that the things that I own do not define me. Almighty God, I am delighted to have You as my Provider.

# SIMPLICITY

*But I fear, lest by any means,*
*as the serpent beguiled Eve through his subtlety,*
*so your minds should be corrupted from the simplicity that is in Christ.*

2 CORINTHIANS 11:3 KJV

Lord, the management principle known as KISS—"Keep It Simple, Stupid"—does have its merit, despite the "Stupid" reference. I am involved in far too many organizations and other activities that fritter away my time and litter my mind. When did I agree to associate with so many organizations? Why did I subscribe to so many magazines? How many hobbies does one person need?

Father, I long for simplicity in my relationship with You. Please help me manage my time so I can focus on a better kinship with You. Release me from the clutter of unimportant activities that infringe on my time and attention.

Lord, I will monitor the activities of my children so that they do not become overloaded with activities that intrude on their time to grow spiritually. I pray that we will make quiet time for reflection and quality time for communicating with You.

# ACTION

*Little children, let us love, not in word or speech,*
*but in truth and action.*

1 JOHN 3:18 NRSV

Dear Father, I pray that I will never be satisfied with myself or become comfortable in my situation. May my contentment be one of action instead of ease. Often responsibilities to my wife and children require prompt and decisive action. I must not be lured into inaction as a crisis develops.

Lord, I ask You to show me the doors of opportunity that I can open to grow and improve. Should I refuse to open those doors, then jar me out of my routine and force me out of my comfort zone. When I see what needs to be done, may I willingly make the effort to do it.

Father, I often see that change is necessary for me to improve. If I do exactly the same thing each day in exactly the same way, then I should not expect results any different from the day before. Help me push beyond the mundane into the realm of active service.

# RESPONSIBILITY

*"God is exalted in his power.*
*Who is a teacher like him?"*

JOB 36:22 NIV

Lord, the opportunity to shape young lives is both a blessing and an awesome responsibility. Show me how to admonish, correct, and inspire those who look to me for guidance. Although I have opportunities to give advice to a variety of individuals at work, at church, and in the community, my greatest desire is to guide the minds of my children. Help me build relationships founded on trust.

Lord, no one teaches like You. Regardless of the circumstances, I will ground my advice on Your Word. Give me the dedication and calm self-assurance to help the people I am mentoring to realize the higher objectives for their lives. As a father, my influence will persist through the lives of my children. I pray that they will have the conviction to remain on course when I am no longer guiding them.

# LIVING THE LIFE

*For thou, Lord, art good, and ready to forgive;*
*and plenteous in mercy unto all them that call upon thee.*

PSALM 86:5 KJV

Lord, it is easy to justify my own mistakes. Yet I find it difficult to ignore the shortcomings of others. When I am late getting ready, it is always for a good reason. But when my children delay getting ready and miss the bus, I lecture them on their indifference to their responsibilities. I have heard that ten praises are needed for every one criticism. Often, I provide the opposite.

Father, I can always detect problems in others more easily than in myself. That is the way my thinking goes, and I know it is not right. Help me to stop being reproachful of others while excusing my own inadequacy. Help me learn to weave my counsel into the fabric of my own life so others can see it.

With Your help, I will show my family and others the same tolerance You have shown me. By forgiving others, I accept Your free grace.

# TEAMWORK

*As every man hath received the gift,*
*even so minister the same one to another,*
*as good stewards of the manifold grace of God.*

1 PETER 4:10 KJV

Lord Most High, I sometimes allow my future to be determined by others. I become dependent upon them to guide me and take the lead in overcoming my problems. At other times, I try to be totally independent of others and chart my own course. I fail to recognize that You have made human beings to be interdependent. I understand this concept as it applies to the church, to my marriage, and to my family.

Lord, may I also recognize the advantages of shared action in my daily contact with other people. By exchanging ideas and working together, we'll be more effective.

I pray that I do not think that in order for me to win, others must lose. Instead, guide me to succeed in cooperative endeavors that bring glory to Your kingdom. Bless my children with a spirit of teamwork. Let them use the gifts You have given them to benefit others.

# CHOICES

*I press on toward the goal to win the prize for
which God has called me heavenward in Christ Jesus.*

PHILIPPIANS 3:14 NIV

Father, last year a friend and I set out to hike a mountain trail. We had no particular destination in mind. The grueling trail ended in a field of boulders and an impassable bank of snow. Later, we learned of a different route that would have taken us to a spectacular vista at the summit.

Lord, I often expend my strength to reach an unworthy goal. The end result is often disappointing. My aim in life is to honor You. Guide me to make good decisions at work and at home. Help me to focus on the spiritual goals that will honor You.

Father, teach me how to use my time and resources wisely so I will be a good example for my children. Help me guide them so they will make excellent choices for their lives and strive for worthy goals.

# PERSISTENCE

*For everything that was written in the past was written to teach us,*
*so that through endurance and the encouragement*
*of the Scriptures we might have hope.*

ROMANS 15:4 NIV

Father, I often battle my computer, especially when installing a new peripheral. Nothing seems to work the first time! I change the data cable, plug it into a different port, reinstall the software, load new drivers, and even read the manual to learn the correct menu choices and commands. Eventually, it works.

Lord, every day I learn the effectiveness of persistence. I encounter problems that at first resist all of my efforts to overcome. But persistence prevails when all else fails. The greatest resistance by the forces against me comes at the moment before success.

Father, I see people who show simple persistence every day—the heroism of working at a thankless job, the endurance of a parent who must repeat the same tasks every day, the determination of a teenager to overcome physical or mental limitations. Grant me persistence and a steadfast singleness of purpose in raising my children and leading my family.

# PURSUANCE

*We sent Timothy, our brother and co-worker for God in proclaiming
the gospel of Christ, to strengthen and encourage you for the sake of
your faith, so that no one would be shaken by these persecutions.*

1 THESSALONIANS 3:2−3 NRSV

Father, I enjoy reading about great achievers in world
history—statesmen, scientists, missionaries, and explorers.
Many were people of exceptional courage, endurance, and
intelligence. Yet my greatest admiration is for common people in
extraordinary circumstances. They stepped out in faith and did what
was required of them. Often, they did not seem to have great
courage, but were willing to overcome their fears for a noble
purpose. They were surprisingly eloquent, not in their words,
but in their lives.

Lord, may I pursue worthy goals as an outgrowth of my
Christian values. I desire to first establish in my heart the right
choices and then follow them in my everyday life despite adversity.
I pray that I will remain faithful to those values and be willing to
submerge my own will to do Your will.

Father, help me steer my children toward real heroes, those who
pursue righteousness. Encourage my children to be heroic in
upholding the values that reflect Your will.

# RESOLUTION

*But Daniel purposed in his heart that he would not*
*defile himself with the portion of the king's meat,*
*nor with the wine which he drank:*
*therefore he requested of the prince of the eunuchs*
*that he might not defile himself.*

DANIEL 1:8 KJV

Heavenly Father, despite the quiet time my family is experiencing now, I know that challenges will test each one of us—if not later today, then sometime soon. Once temptations come, I seldom have adequate time or the proper environment to make a reasoned response. My goal is to look ahead and consider the evils I will face and make the right decision before the events occur. I wish also to foresee challenges my children will encounter and prepare them for those tests.

I pray that the choices I make will provide an example to my children so that they, too, will have the courage to choose truth over lies, courage over flight, righteousness over evil.

After I make an important decision, there is a time of second-guessing, both from myself and from others. Rid my mind of these doubts that serve no useful end. I pray I will be resolute and boldly live a consistent, purposeful life.

# WISDOM

*The mouths of the righteous utter wisdom, and their tongues speak justice.*
*The law of their God is in their hearts; their steps do not slip.*

PSALM 37:30–31 NRSV

Father, my knowledge is limited and my ignorance is endless. Even when I know what should be done, I sometimes am faint of heart. I hesitate because I realize that my decisions often have consequences that will have major effects on my family.

Lord, I will never know enough to always make the right choices on my own. I pray that You will give me the wisdom to choose what is right and lasting. Give me the good sense to correctly discern the choices that keep me in agreement with Your eternal plan.

Father, let me show that I have Your blessing by leading an honorable and acceptable life. It is not always apparent to others that the best course of action is one in keeping with Your direction. Help me have the courage to act upon the wisdom that You have generously given me.

# SOVEREIGNTY OF GOD

*Thou hast made me as the clay. . . . Thou hast clothed me
with skin and flesh, and hast fenced me with bones and sinews.
Thou hast granted me life and favour,
and thy visitation hath preserved my spirit.*

JOB 10:9, 11–12 KJV

Father, as I hold my newborn daughter, I acknowledge her as Your gift to me. I accept Your sovereignty over her, and I ask for Your providential care. I pray for Your loving provision for all her needs.

Lord, I intend to set a godly example for my daughter. My goal is to lead her to You. I pray that she chooses to give allegiance to Your rule. Although I will raise her, care for her, and provide her with a Christian home, she will eventually be at the age to make her own choices. I cannot envision what would make her rebel against the love given to her.

Father, in the same way, You have been with me, cared for me, and provided me with the best things in my life. I am drawn to Your love. I pray that I will always be mindful of those blessings and always keep myself fully planted in Your sovereignty.

# PEACE

*"You will be secure, because there is hope;
you will look about you and take your rest in safety.
You will lie down, with no one to make you afraid,
and many will court your favor."*

JOB 11:18–19 NIV

Father, at bedtime I talked to my young daughter about the events of the day, listened as she said her prayers, and tucked the blanket around her. As I closed the door, she pulled her stuffed rabbit closer and settled down in the glow of the night-light. She fell asleep almost before I whispered, "Good night."

Lord, I realize that her peaceful sleep came from a feeling of comfort and security. If there had been unexpected sounds or unfamiliar surroundings, she would not have gone to sleep as quickly. But her mother and I try to provide her with the conditions that make her feel protected.

Father, a feeling of security is important at any age. I recognize Your strength as my protection. With the comfort of Your Word, I can put my daily concerns behind me. Thank You, Lord, for giving me the assurance of Your love and protection.

## SELF-RESPECT

*Do you not know that your body is a temple of the Holy Spirit,*
*who is in you, whom you have received from God?*
*You are not your own; you were bought at a price.*
*Therefore honor God with your body.*

1 CORINTHIANS 6:19–20 NIV

Dear Father, I want to help my daughter develop the important attributes of self-respect, self-worth, and a positive sense of purpose. Help me recognize her talents and provide her the opportunity to develop them. Prompt me to express my delight at her efforts. Remind me to put on display her artwork and awards. I have heard that ten positive comments are required for every negative one. Help me spend far more time honoring her achievements than discussing her failures.

Lord, I want to help her become aware of her beliefs and values. Once those are clear, she will be less likely to compromise those values because that would diminish her self-respect.

Father, the Bible is filled with examples about our worth. You created us, You sacrificed Your Son for us, and You were too kind to leave us without the comfort of the Holy Spirit. In every aspect, You have shown our value. Guide me as I build self-respect in my daughter.

# ESSENCE

*May the grace of the Lord Jesus Christ, and the love of God,
and the fellowship of the Holy Spirit be with you all.*

2 CORINTHIANS 13:14 NIV

Father, I have heard that a young man can get some idea of how his wife will relate to him by watching how she relates to her father. In that case, the man who marries my daughter will have a wonderful wife.

Lord, when she was small, she walked with me, and she could hardly reach high enough to grasp my hand. Now we can walk side by side. As she grew taller, she also grew in spiritual stature. I appreciate my daughter as much as I did when she was little. She has grown, changed, and gained confidence. Yet her essence is still that of a loving, considerate, and thoughtful daughter.

Father, as she leaves for college, keep her safe. I pray she continues to follow the guidance of the Holy Spirit in the ways of righteousness. Provide her with the inner strength to remain true to those things that her mother and I have taught her.

# VITAL

*Godliness has value for all things,*
*holding promise for both the present life and the life to come.*

1 TIMOTHY 4:8 NIV

Father, when I was young, children would excuse their failures or belittle someone else's successes by saying, "In a hundred years no one will remember this." Actually, the comment does allow me to contrast trivial and important matters. Significant actions and comments have a way of reaching beyond the present and affecting eternity.

Lord, because of my limited understanding, I am not always certain of what is worthy of serious attention. Guide me to always take seriously my responsibility to dedicate my words and actions to You. Use what I say and do to influence someone to spend eternity with You. Today, I trust that I have done all I could to accomplish that goal.

Father, guide me as my children learn how to distinguish between what is trivial and what is vital. Help me teach them to focus their lives on actions that will have eternal value.

# MASTER

*A son honors his father, and servants their master.*
*If then I am a father, where is the honor due me?*
*And if I am a master, where is the respect due me?*
*says the LORD of hosts to you.*

MALACHI 1:6 NRSV

Lord, I know of a bronze statue in Edinburgh, Scotland, that commemorates a Skye terrier named Greyfriars Bobby. After his owner died, this dog followed the funeral procession to the churchyard where they buried his master. The terrier stayed near his grave for the next fourteen years.

Divine Master, You not only died, but You died because of my sins. I want to dedicate my life to You. I will show my loyalty to You by being faithful to Your church and devoted to my family. My eyes will remain fixed on Calvary. Your cross demonstrates the truth that You will never leave me or forsake me.

Lord, give me a heart to be wholly committed to You as my Master. I actively dedicate myself to Your service. Build in me the strength for dedication that lasts beyond a few days or weeks and becomes a lifelong loyalty to my family and You.

# QUALIFIED

*I therefore, the prisoner of the Lord,
beseech you that ye walk worthy of the vocation
wherewith ye are called.*

EPHESIANS 4:1 KJV

Father, I am impressed when I watch a skilled carpenter or auto mechanic at work. I am struck by how they select a tool that is perfectly fitted for the task at hand.

Dear Lord, I see that You have given me particular skills and abilities. Others can fill in for me should I not do the jobs for which I have been created. However, You have called me into service to apply my unique talents to those tasks that I can do best. May I never evade my responsibilities by claiming that someone else is better qualified.

Father, I pray that I can help my children recognize their particular talents and give them the guidance to enhance those talents. I pray that they will happily accept the responsibility to serve others in the way You have equipped them. May they learn from me the joy of Christian service.

## COMPELLED

*Yet when I preach the gospel, I cannot boast,*
*for I am compelled to preach.*
*Woe to me if I do not preach the gospel!*

1 CORINTHIANS 9:16 NIV

Father, I desire my children to be strong in character and commendable in their actions. I want them to be dedicated to doing their best. I am gratified when their teachers inform me that they are both intelligent and have practical ability. It is great to find that a child can be trusted to be truthful and honest. I pray that my children develop high moral standards and become good role models for their friends to look up to. Yet their accomplishments are lacking if they are not brought to the feet of Jesus and embrace Him as their Savior.

Lord, I know that I have a duty to spread the gospel. Although actions speak louder than words, actions without words are not enough. Help me become dedicated to the gospel, compelled to tell others about the salvation found only in Jesus. Let me start at home, so that my children realize that success is not complete until they have become Your children.

## INSTRUCTION

*No discipline seems pleasant at the time, but painful.*
*Later on, however, it produces a harvest of righteousness*
*and peace for those who have been trained by it.*

HEBREWS 12:11 NIV

Father, during one of my periodic attempts to improve my golf game, an instructor watched my swing and offered advice. His greatest concern was with my grip. He showed me the proper way to place my thumb and fingers. He insisted I use the new grip, although I found it uncomfortable at first.

Lord, I recognize that discipline is training that alters a person's behavior for the better. May I always use discipline to instruct, train, and teach my children. Give me the temperament to handle anger so that anger and punishment do not become part of my discipline. May my discipline always be moderated with affection.

Father, it is difficult to overcome early training that is bad, and it is difficult to go against early training that is good. Help me give proper training that will last a lifetime. Allow me to show my children the proof of my love for them through discipline that sets their lives on the proper course.

# TESTS

*Test everything. Hold on to the good.*

1 THESSALONIANS 5:21 NIV

Father, while going through school, teachers were always giving tests to students. I didn't like taking exams, but they did make me study the information being taught and motivate me to learn. Without periodic checks on my progress, I would have become careless in my studies and uncertain of my real mastery of the subject.

Lord, may I not become lax in learning more about You and living a life pleasing to You. When I am tested, help me make the choices that will lead to victory. As my children face decisions about proper spiritual choices, give me the talent to assist them when it is necessary and the wisdom to let them test their own mettle when it is appropriate.

Father, throughout life I encounter choices that challenge me. As I examine each situation, I pray that my desire will be to do what is right, and You will give me the strength to stand by my choice.

# GEMS

*Ye also, as lively stones, are built up a spiritual house,*
*an holy priesthood, to offer up spiritual sacrifices,*
*acceptable to God by Jesus Christ.*

1 PETER 2:5 KJV

Lord, when I walk along a fast flowing stream or stand at the beach as the waves roll in, I am amazed at the ceaseless action of the water. I find stones that are rounded smooth by the continuous pounding of the water. Even the edges of broken glass are smoothed away until they are no longer sharp.

Father, I see Your ceaseless action in my life in the same way. Day by day, You remove my rough edges. You blunt my sharp tongue, soften my overbearing manner, cool my hot temper, and smooth out my uneven disposition. From a rough and unremarkable stone, You have made me into something better. Thank You for continuously changing me.

Heavenly Father, my children are also rough stones, but they have the potential to be gems. I pray I'll expose them to the right actions that will improve their character. Shape them into citizens of Your heavenly kingdom.

## CONSEQUENCES

*Because the LORD disciplines those he loves,*
*as a father the son he delights in.*

PROVERBS 3:12 NIV

Father, I have many roles in my position as the head of my family. I approach discipline with more trepidation than any other aspect of being a father. Most discipline is training—guiding the young one toward a specific goal. I put rules in place to ensure that my children do not stray too far from the expected pattern for their lives. But occasionally, the rules are intentionally broken and consequences must be exacted.

Lord, help me choose realistic expectations and state them clearly. Give me the wisdom to set the consequences appropriate to the age of the child. A two-minute time-out is an eternity for a small child. A two-week loss of the phone is forever for a teenager. Despite their pleadings and objections, help me enforce the consequences of the rules I have set. Afterward, I pray that my children recognize the discipline as an indication of my love for them.

# REVITALIZE

*"But charge Joshua, and encourage and strengthen him,*
*because it is he who shall cross over at the head of this people*
*and who shall secure their possession of the land that you will see."*
DEUTERONOMY 3:28 NRSV

Father, You instructed Moses to encourage Joshua to lead
Your people across the Jordan River into the Promised
Land. In the same way, help me encourage those who have
been chosen to serve. Help me ease their burdens and give them the
will to continue the work You have called them to do.

Lord, when I am leading my family, may I always be mindful of
my role as Your servant. Help me choose the right words and
actions to revitalize my wife and children when they have grown
weary, assure them when they have doubts, console
them in times of apparent failure, and reward them
with heartfelt praise for their successes. May I never
ask them to do what I am unwilling to do myself.
Father, grant me the ability to choose
what is right and give me the ability to
persuade others to make that
choice, too.

# REFRESHED

*"I know your deeds, your love and faith, your service and perseverance,
and that you are now doing more than you did at first."*

REVELATION 2:19 NIV

Father, when I awake each morning, I am rested, refreshed, and ready to meet the challenges of the new day. But such a positive outlook is difficult to maintain all day long. When I become spiritually low, I am reminded to renew myself with You. I need to draw from the storehouse of Your love.

Lord, I look back through all of my experiences and see the ways that You have provided for my needs every day. You loved me when I was still a sinner, pardoned me by the blood of Jesus, and welcomed me as one of Your children. I thank You for all I have, especially the gift of my wife and children.

Father, I ask not for easier tasks but for better ability to meet the assignments You give me. Refresh me daily with Your strength and love, and give me the loving nature that can help ease the burdens of others.

# SPEED

*He restoreth my soul:*
*he leadeth me in the paths of righteousness for his name's sake.*
*Yea, though I walk through the valley of the shadow of death,*
*I will fear no evil: for thou art with me;*
*thy rod and thy staff they comfort me.*

PSALM 23:3−4 KJV

Father, one of the more dangerous sections of highway near my home has been improved. The shoulders are wider, some of the curves have been straightened, and turning lanes have been added. Before the changes, driving errors could lead to disaster. But now, the likelihood of accidents has been reduced. However, I drive faster on the new section, speeding along where I used to drive with more caution.

Lord, I am aware that You have made improvements in my life. Thank You for taking care of the spiritual and physical dangers as they occur along the road of my life. I pray that I will not use the smoother path for speeding along without paying attention to the many blessings You have given me. I pray that I will never go faster than Your guidance. Help me to direct my children to put their trust in You, too. Only You can see the evil and temptations that lie ahead waiting to wreck a life.

# KEEPING IN TUNE

*"For my yoke is easy, and my burden is light."*
MATTHEW 11:30 NRSV

Father, while visiting a pioneer village with my children, we watched a blacksmith making horseshoes. First, he heated an iron bar until it was white-hot. Then he held it against an anvil with long pliers. With his other arm he swung the heavy hammer. To shape the horseshoe, he moved the iron bar but kept the hammer going at a steady pace, as if playing a tune. The blacksmith could work for hours because he let the hammer have its way.

Father, serving You becomes far less exhausting by being in tune with Your will. Weariness develops when I try to interpret Your will to meet my goals. Lord, help me grasp the advantages of keeping in tune with Your decrees, and help me teach this important concept to my children, as well. Many of our problems come from trying to bend Your will to our goals. Instead, help us work with You rather than against You.

# CHEER

*These things I have spoken unto you, that in me ye might have peace.*
*In the world ye shall have tribulation: but be of good cheer;*
*I have overcome the world.*

JOHN 16:33 KJV

Father, I watched the coach of my daughter's soccer team. He shouted encouragement at the top of his lungs. When a player missed a shot, he would later take them aside and explain in a gentle voice why they missed the play. Regardless of the score, he kept encouraging his players to do better—and they did. Like the coach, I have learned that encouragement improves performance, while criticism puts a damper on it.

Lord, I am thankful that Your Word is filled with encouragement. Even when You ask us to do the impossible, it becomes possible because we are not acting alone. You are with us, and You help and cheer us on to do better.

Father, at the soccer game, I saw young players scanning the stands looking for their fathers and mothers. When they saw their parents watching, they renewed their efforts. Thank You, Father, for always being with us, watching and encouraging.

## STRENGTH

*Therefore encourage one another and build each other up,*
*just as in fact you are doing.*

1 THESSALONIANS 5:11 NIV

Father, I am continually amazed at the power of encouraging words. While hiking in the Grand Canyon, I saw a park ranger coming to the aid of a hiker who appeared to be totally exhausted. I assumed the individual would need to be airlifted out. Later, I met the park ranger and asked about the hiker. She explained that she had been able to "talk" him out. She suggested that he walk a little farther up the trail to a place with more shade. After a rest, she encouraged him, walked with him, and eventually he made it to the rim of the canyon.

Lord, I know that words are a powerful tool for strengthening people. The right words can build hope, restore confidence, and increase courage. Please give me the right words to inspire my children. Often, the only help I need to give them are words of encouragement.

## BUILDING UP

*Humble yourselves therefore under the mighty hand of God,
so that he may exalt you in due time.
Cast all your anxiety on him, because he cares for you.*

1 PETER 5:6—7 NRSV

Father, I used to sigh at the responsibilities that were imposed on me; now I rejoice that You strengthened me to meet the challenges. At one time I was entangled in the world; now I feel myself liberated by Your love. I used to feel embedded in sin; now I am living in Your affection. Before, I envied those who lived in better circumstances than myself; today, I recognize the blessings of my own prosperity. I feel that You have exalted me. You have raised me above grasping at the mundane so I can reach for greater achievements.

Father, in the same way that You have built my confidence, help me make it possible for my children to face the future with a positive attitude. I want them to go ahead with their plans, never giving undue concern that someone might be against them. Help them learn not to care about trivial distractions and instead concentrate on the vital goals that lead to happiness in a life of service to You.

## SPOKEN LOVE

*The tongue has the power of life and death,*
*and those who love it will eat its fruit.*

PROVERBS 18:21 NIV

Lord, the Bible tells me of the power of Your words. You spoke the world into existence. You spoke a blessing to Abraham that eventually brought Your Son to Earth. Help me realize that my words are powerful, too, especially when addressing my children. I pray that I may never speak disparaging about them. But more importantly, I pray that I bless them with encouragement.

Father, sometimes I feel awkward trying to express my support for them in a meaningful way. Help me reinforce the power of my love and Your love by telling my children that they are special to me and to You. I pray that I'll be able to help them recognize and use the gifts You have given them. As they grow older, I pray for Your divine favor on their enterprises. May they always have faithful, loving, forgiving, and generous spirits.

## STAMINA

*Therefore, since we are surrounded by such a great cloud of witnesses,*
*let us throw off everything that hinders and the sin that so easily entangles,*
*and let us run with perseverance the race marked out for us.*

HEBREWS 12:1 NIV

Father, I admire those individuals who show the endurance to complete difficult races that last for days. A great adventure takes long preparation, and sometimes people drop out even before the contest begins. Only a few make it to the starting line, and even fewer complete the race.

Lord, I think of the pioneers who crossed featureless deserts and climbed through heart-pounding mountain passes. They set out on the journey with the hope that a better life awaited them.

Father, help my family and me to realize that life is more like a marathon than a sprint. Give us the endurance to train for, enter, and complete the race. We need to wisely prepare for the race with all the equipment You have provided. In the Spirit, we will climb over mountain peaks, trek across desert valleys, and surmount other obstacles. And we are not alone; You are with us.

# THRIVING

*I will praise thee, O LORD, with my whole heart;*
*I will show forth all thy marvellous works.*
*I will be glad and rejoice in thee:*
*I will sing praise to thy name,*
*O thou most High.*

PSALM 9:1–2 KJV

ear Lord, during the early morning of a day I spent in the desert, insects crawled into the blossoms of a hedge-hog cactus. At midday, a red-tailed hawk rested on a tall saguaro and watched for an incautious lizard to dart from its shade beneath a rock. Late in the evening, I observed a hungry coyote eating fruit that had dropped to the ground from a date palm.

Lord, I watched in fascination as life managed to survive and even thrive despite the harsh environment. I rejoiced in the wonder that I saw in Your created Earth. The plants and animals survived because they are Your special creation, and You equipped them with the traits they need for their life in the desert.

Father God, help me understand that You have equipped me with everything I need to live as Your child. May my family and I also survive and thrive in Your love.

## STRIVING

*This is a trustworthy saying that deserves full acceptance
(and for this we labor and strive), that we have put our hope
in the living God, who is the Savior of all men,
and especially of those who believe.*

1 TIMOTHY 4:9–10 NIV

Father, spring is a time of growth and renewal, a time of new life and hope. This spring, an astonishing sight greeted me as I walked along a recently built walkway. A spring flower had managed to push through the hard asphalt. The delicate sprout had displayed unusual power as it shoved aside the heavy material that blocked its way to sunlight.

Lord, I am often surprised to see children who have managed to survive and even thrive despite the most difficult home life and adverse circumstances. Dedicated Christians have planted Your love in their hearts. These children show the amazing resilience of those who strive to reach Your love. I pray that I give to my children the desire to always reach toward You.

Father, I want to daily renew myself spiritually. I pray that I will manifest strength of character to overcome those forces that get in my way of growing in Your light.

# PATIENCE

*Therefore, as God's chosen people, holy and dearly loved,*
*clothe yourselves with compassion, kindness,*
*humility, gentleness and patience.*

COLOSSIANS 3:12 NIV

Dear Father, impatience is one of my faults. I am intolerant of delay at work, irritated when family members do not share my urgency, and restless in the face of inaction. Patience is an attribute that I need in double measure as a father. I need the patience for everyday delays as well as long-term patience as my children develop the maturity to make intelligent decisions.

Lord, I also need to learn patience with You. Sometimes I impatiently decide You are not going to solve a problem, and I act outside Your will. I make ill-considered decisions and take reckless actions that endanger me physically and spiritually.

Father, I trust in You. I pray that Your inner peace will sustain me. My goal is neither the impatience of rash actions nor the inaction of passive resignation but the endurance of a mature Christian who perseveres while awaiting Your will.

# VALUES

*I pray that the God of our Lord Jesus Christ, the Father of glory,*
*may give you a spirit of wisdom and revelation as you come to know him.*

EPHESIANS 1:17 NRSV

Father, I hear the word *family* used in a variety of ways today. Television has the family hour, which is for family-oriented shows, although they often are not. Some families designate a space in their home as a family room but seldom use it except for watching television. The term *family man* may merely mean a man who has a wife and children.

Lord, I pray that I live up to the term *family man* to the full extent of its meaning. I pray that under Your leadership, I will build a strong family on the rock of Your wisdom.

Father, may my family and I develop shared Christian goals and spiritual values. May we have a long-term commitment to one another and to You. After my children become adults, may they still reside under the tent of Your blessings.

# ILLUMINATE

*But you, beloved, are not in darkness, for that day to surprise you
like a thief; for you are all children of light and children of the day;
we are not of the night or of darkness.*

1 THESSALONIANS 5:4—5 NRSV

L ord, the other night during a power failure, I was the first
to find a flashlight. The little light was enough to dispel
the darkness. Because I carried the light, members of my
family gathered around me.

Father, I recognize one of my roles is to be a light to my children.
I need to illuminate the proper choices in their lives—the righteous
choices. I must be firm, with a resolute will, yet not overbearing.

Lord, Your radiance illuminates all creation, yet I see people
stumbling in spiritual gloom. Although I am but a pale reflection of
Your brilliance, I pray that the teaching I do becomes a beacon that
draws lost souls into the circle of Your light. May my light never
dazzle but reveal. Guide me so that I push out the darkness and fill
the lives of others with the light of Christ.

# PRECIOUS

*For he says, "At an acceptable time I have listened to you,*
*and on a day of salvation I have helped you."*
*See, now is the acceptable time; see,*
*now is the day of salvation!*

2 CORINTHIANS 6:2 NRSV

Father, I am fascinated by time-travel stories. Going back to reexperience a pleasant event or to correct a decision that led to disaster is an idea that I find attractive. Of course, it is impossible to go back in time and undo events. Time is a one-way street.

Lord, Your Word begins with a mention of time, "In the beginning," and ends with a mention of time, "Surely I am coming soon." I see my journey on Earth as aboard a time machine that can only move forward. I must give my best efforts the first time.

Father, I wish to use well the time You have given me. I must wisely decide what is the best use of my time. But help me recognize that time is too precious to waste pursuing what many in the world think of as success. Instead, direct me to invest my time to develop closer harmony with my family and with You.

## SCHOOL

*A wise man will hear, and will increase learning;*
*and a man of understanding shall attain unto wise counsels.*

PROVERBS 1:5 KJV

Heavenly Father, as part of my duties as a parent, I deal with the schools that my children attend. In many instances, the procedures and policies seem to require a considerable capacity for patience. Please equip me with that patience and with the insight to help improve the education of my children and other students, as well.

I pray that our educators have the ability to motivate children to their best achievement. Provide our teachers with the means to instill in students a joy for learning and the capacity for a lifetime of seeking the truth. Develop in our teachers and students boldness to express their love for You.

Revive our education system so teachers and students can express their Christian beliefs. May teachers be able to show the religious context that guided the founding of our great nation. May teachers be a role model of excellence and integrity.

## GOALS OF A FATHER

*For you know that we dealt with each of you as a father deals with
his own children, encouraging, comforting and urging you to live
lives worthy of God, who calls you into his kingdom and glory.*

1 THESSALONIANS 2:11−12 NIV

Heavenly Father, I am perplexed by how the world sees
fathers. In the old television shows, the man of the house
was a wise, successful, and morally superior man. Today,
the father is often portrayed as a bewildered but loveable buffoon without the foggiest notion of how to solve the problems his children face.

Lord, as a father I want to provide affection and emotional support. Help me communicate in a way that they can understand. May I
give training in proper behavior and supply a gentle but constant
pressure for them to develop to their highest capabili-
ties. Help my children understand that my success in
training them requires responsibilities on their part, too.
As my children grow, I want them to gain the
wisdom to remember and emulate the good
things that they saw in my life. Even
when my children are not present, I
desire that my actions be those of a
godly father. Most important of all,
I want to be the cornerstone of a righteous family.

# OPEN LINE

*Listen, children, to a father's instruction, and be attentive,*
*that you may gain insight; for I give you good precepts:*
*do not forsake my teaching.*

PROVERBS 4:1–2 NRSV

I f my children are away on Mother's Day they call their mother, and on Father's Day they call me, too—collect. If they are home on Mother's Day, they take us out to eat, and I pay. On Father's Day they take us out to eat, too—and I pay. But I do get to enjoy conversation with my children.

Lord, help me make it plain to my children that they have an open line of communication to me and that I will be there in time of crisis. I pray they also realize that I will listen when they simply wish to pass the time of day.

Father God, I think of the times that I have put in collect calls to You. I know You are happy to receive my prayers, regardless of the circumstances. I pray that I will be an example of a loving, patient father like You.

# CHECKLIST

*He hath shown thee, O man, what is good;*
*and what doth the LORD require of thee,*
*but to do justly, and to love mercy,*
*and to walk humbly with thy God?*

MICAH 6:8 KJV

Father, my company is big on checklists. I must go through a sequence of steps before I can start a complex piece of equipment. Sometimes I am surprised at what I find: a fuel gauge that reads inaccurately, a switch left on by the previous operator, a stuck valve, or a safety shield that is missing.

Lord, I pray that I will take my duties as a father as seriously as I do when working around heavy equipment. Help me constantly examine what is required of me to avoid physical or spiritual injury to those under my care. I will teach honesty by keeping promises that I make to my family. I will exercise courage when others try to intimidate me. I will show justice by being fair with everyone. I will demonstrate respect by treating my family with love and deference. I will model obedience by reading and following Your teachings.

## SEASONS OF LIFE

*There is a time for everything,*
*and a season for every activity under heaven:*
*a time to be born and a time to die.*

ECCLESIASTES 3:1−2 NIV

Father, each year as I watch the seasons unfold, I become more aware of the changes in my life. I see the growth of spring foliage, the nearly imperceptible change in the larger trees from year to year, then the appearance of fall colors. Later in the year when I find frost on my windshield, I become aware that the growing season has ended and that cold weather will soon grip the land.

Lord, as the years have slipped away, I realize that my children are in their final preparations to leave home. I sometimes resist the changes that their greater maturity brings. But change is a part of Your design. You created the seasons for healthy growth, and change must take place in my family, too.

Heavenly Father, it is time for my children to seek their own way. I pray that the way they seek and the path they find is in keeping with Your will.

# UNITY

*And the glory which thou gavest me I have given them;*
*that they may be one, even as we are one.*

JOHN 17:22 KJV

Righteous Father, I am humbled when I realize that Jesus, on the night He was betrayed, prayed for unity of believers. I look at Your Word through different eyes than other Christians and often cannot fully agree with them. But help me focus on our many vital common beliefs rather than our few trivial differences. Help me see the strength in unity and the danger in discord.

Lord, thank You for giving my family the blessing of fellowship with believers. In our unity with others, we are strengthened. Our joy is renewed, and we grow in knowledge and understanding of Your will.

Father, often it is easy to agree if the agreement is to do nothing. Let my agreement be to act and do, not sit back and wait. Let me join the fellowship of believers so we become a force for righteousness—Jesus would want it.

# FORWARD

*So we fix our eyes not on what is seen, but on what is unseen.*
*For what is seen is temporary, but what is unseen is eternal.*

2 CORINTHIANS 4:18 NIV

Father, as my daughter completed her driving training course, she reported that the best advice she received was to look ahead in the distance. The car took a straighter course, and she could control it better if she looked where it was going, not where it was.

Lord, I recall the words of Leroy (Satchel) Paige, "Don't look back. Something may be gaining on you." This principle is useful in my life. In my day-to-day living, some circumstances often seem to engulf me. But if I look at the point where I intend to go, not at my present position, it becomes clearer what I should do.

Father, I know that it is impossible to know what the future holds. I cannot direct my own way. That is the reason that I must depend on You. I pray that I will center my objectives on being in fellowship with You.

# BELIEVERS

*Let us not give up meeting together, as some are in the habit of doing,*
*but let us encourage one another—and all the more*
*as you see the Day approaching.*

HEBREWS 10:25 NIV

Heavenly Father, reading the Bible, talking to You in prayer, singing hymns, and meeting with other Christians help fortify my spiritual life. Only by becoming strong in You can I overcome obstacles. I need to assemble with other Christians because I gain strength by associating with those who love You.

Lord, help my children feel blessed to have the opportunity to gather with other Christians. Singing, praying, and studying Your Word will inspire them to a closer walk with You. May they always be glad to participate with other believers in strengthening one another and in worshiping You.

Father, I, too, need the fellowship of dedicated believers. I pray that I lead my entire family to take advantage of every opportunity to attend church services. May we worship and glorify You. Help me realize that we are blessed through fellowship with others.

## CAMARADERIE

*Therefore, as God's chosen people, holy and dearly loved, clothe yourselves
with compassion, kindness, humility, gentleness and patience.
Bear with each other and forgive whatever grievances you may have
against one another. Forgive as the Lord forgave you. And over all these
virtues put on love, which binds them all together in perfect unity.*

COLOSSIANS 3:12–14 NIV

Father, I have heard fellowship described as "fellows in the
same ship." They willingly work together because the success of their voyage depends upon mutual trust and a feeling
of kinship.

Lord, my family and I are working with other Christians toward
common goals of living justly, walking humbly, and loving mercy.
Because all Christians share these goals, help me recognize a common
fellowship.

Father, help me embrace all
Christians as my brothers and
sisters because we have an
underlying oneness with You.
We share the same faith and
the same hope. Create a desire
in me to embrace them with
love and kinship. We are truly
fellows in the same ship.

# ANGER

*Those with good sense are slow to anger,*
*and it is their glory to overlook an offense.*

PROVERBS 19:11 NRSV

Father, my children can be an object lesson in how I should deal with my anger. I notice that a child's anger is short lived. Two little friends can have a disagreement, and within a brief time they are playing together again.

Lord, I realize that anger and forgiveness cannot exist together. Only after I rid myself of my anger can I begin the process of forgiveness. Anger and a peaceful mind are mutually exclusive, too, because I cannot have a loving and calm mind when resentment is present. Anger not only keeps me from feeling love for the target of my hostility, but it prevents me from loving others, as well. When I rage against another person, everything else is pushed aside.

Father, I pray that I learn not only to control my anger but also how to diffuse it and rid my mind of it. May I be an example for my family by putting anger in its place.

# REMOVE

*As far as the east is from the west,*
*so far hath he removed our transgressions from us.*
*Like as a father pitieth his children,*
*so the LORD pitieth them that fear him.*

PSALM 103:12—13 KJV

Father, I am always making mistakes. As a child, I used an eraser to rub out the errors and correct them, although the erasures were obvious on the paper. More recently, I used touch-up paint to cover scratches on door frames, but getting the paints to match exactly was impossible. Errors can never be completely concealed.

Lord, I often see how my children try to hide a problem. What they claimed was a clean bedroom often had trash stowed under the bed. Once, they glued a broken vase back together to pass as undamaged, but the repair failed to fool anyone.

Father, I sometimes make bad judgments and sin against You. Within my own power, I cannot correct them, but I trust in Jesus to blot out all iniquities. When You remove them, You don't leave a smudgy erasure or a mismatched touch-up. Thank You for removing them entirely so they no longer exist.

# INJUSTICES

*"Whenever you stand praying, forgive,*
*if you have anything against anyone;*
*so that your Father in heaven may also forgive you your trespasses."*

MARK 11:25 NRSV

Sometimes, Lord, my mind wanders back to my earlier life. For some reason, injustices immediately come to mind more readily than pleasant experiences. Anger surfaces when I dwell on the unfair treatment I have experienced. I had many privileged opportunities and blessings, but I remember the negative events with far more emotion than the positive occasions.

Father, I recall a saying that I saw on a sundial: "I count only the sunny hours." I see this attitude in my young children who quickly replace the howls of being slighted with songs of happiness. Help me develop an attitude that focuses on my blessings.

Forgiving Lord, help me press on with my life. Reviewing reruns of my past serves no purpose. I shall not use past events as an excuse for my current shortcomings. With Your help, I will release the resentments I have carried so long and accept responsibility for my own actions.

# UNCONDITIONAL

*My offenses will be sealed up in a bag;*
*you will cover over my sin.*

JOB 14:17 NIV

Father, my life is often in shambles because I fail to follow Your good guidance. I ask Your forgiveness. Thank You for the gift of Your Son who, through His sacrifice, gives reconciliation and mercy. Continue to deal gently with me.

Lord, I participate in Your forgiveness through my forgiveness of others. There is no limit to Your forgiveness of me, so there should be no limit to my forgiveness of others. Grant me the ability to renounce anger and resentment against those who have hurt me. I know it is impossible for me to do this on my own, but through You I have the ability to do the impossible. You excuse my faults without demanding punishment. Give me the grace to do the same for others.

Father, I pardon to the extent that I love, and I love my children dearly. Let them see the extent of my love through my forgiveness.

# BEFORE AND AFTER

*Even before a word is on my tongue,*
*O LORD, you know it completely.*
*You hem me in, behind and before, and lay your hand upon me.*

PSALM 139:4—5 NRSV

F ather, when my daughter began to crawl, her mother and I were always there, picking up what she had dropped and setting straight what she turned over. But we also went before her, making sure she could not pull something down on herself. We put away those items too dangerous to be in her hands. We prepared a safe play area for her.

Lord, as my daughter grew older, we gave her help without her being aware of it. A little child who leaves toys strewn around needs our help in putting them away. An older child leaves a series of events that needs straightened out, too. Just as importantly as when she was smaller, we still took steps to smooth the way in advance of her.

Father, I realize now that You are both behind and ahead of me. You not only clean up my mistakes, You also level the path before me. Thank You, Father, for doing all for me, both seen and unseen.

## SURVIVAL

*Nevertheless I am continually with you; you hold my right hand.*
*You guide me with your counsel,*
*and afterward you will receive me with honor.*

PSALM 73:23–24 NRSV

Father, whenever I take my family hiking, I feel more comfortable if I carry a trail guide. But sometimes I put it in my pocket and forget to check the landmarks as we pass them. When the trail divides and I reach a point of decision, I regret that I have not traced my progress more carefully. I not only need to carry a trail guide, I also need to study it as I go.

Heavenly Father, Your Word is my survival guide. When a crisis arises, I turn to the Bible for comfort. But when my study has been lax, I feel like I am on the trail with an inadequately used trail guide. It would have been better to develop the comfort of Your Word before the emergency arose.

Lord, I want to equip my children with the survival traits to avoid having the world overcome them. Help them remember to carry Your trail guide—the Bible—and also read it and make it their guide in all spiritual matters.

# DECISIONS

*Let your speech always be gracious, seasoned with salt,*
*so that you may know how you ought to answer everyone.*

COLOSSIANS 4:6 NRSV

Lord, I often must make decisions that affect others on short notice. Despite complex situations, I must answer "yes" or "no" and do it quickly. The proper course of action is not always obvious because I lack all the facts necessary to make a well-informed choice. Yet I cannot delay because the decision must be made today, not tomorrow.

Father, sometimes my children come to me asking for permission to do some activity. Help me take the time to be better informed about how my decision may affect them. Often, the question arises when other matters distract me. Please help me put my family first, so that my thinking is in focus.

Dear Jesus, I always want my choices to be in keeping with the examples set by You. But when the options appear equally valid, each having risks and benefits, I pray I will be both wise and decisive.

# PERSPECTIVE

*"For the eyes of the Lord are on the righteous,
and his ears are open to their prayer."*

1 PETER 3:12 NRSV

Dear Lord, viewing the world from a thousand feet up in a hot air balloon gives me an unusual perspective. I can see dangerous situations develop before they become obvious to others. I can see that the canoe in the stream will hit rapids around the bend. I can see two cars coming toward one another along a country lane, but because of a hill, the drivers can't see each other. My eyes are no sharper than theirs, but I have a better perspective.

Father, I know You have a better viewpoint. You can see into hearts, and You know what the future holds. You can see situations before they arise in our lives and prepare us for the proper way for us to have a victory over them. Please continue to watch over us. I pray that through the study of Your Word and our prayers for Your guidance, we will be lifted to a better vantage point and will plan our lives according to Your direction.

# BEACON

*"The people who sat in darkness have seen a great light,
and for those who sat in the region
and shadow of death light has dawned."*

MATTHEW 4:16 NRSV

Father, while traveling in the desert country of the southwest, I noticed that some of the older ranches had a tall pole with a lantern on top. I learned that this custom had begun years ago. People would ride away from the ranch during the day and find themselves confused as to the way back after sunset. On a dark, moonless night the landmarks disappeared. They could only find their way back to the safety of the ranch by looking for the beacon.

Lord, although only a pinprick of light in a vast expanse of darkness, the tiny lantern guided the way for the lost travelers. Sometimes one must show the way by active leading. But the beacon guided others merely by letting its light shine at the right place.

Father, I pray that I serve as a beacon for my family. I pray that by recognizing me as a source of guidance, they will find the way to You as the shelter for their lives.

# LISTEN

*My dear brothers, take note of this:*
*Everyone should be quick to listen,*
*slow to speak and slow to become angry.*

JAMES 1:19 NIV

Lord, I study to improve my skills as a father. Sometimes this training merely makes me feel bad because after learning what I should do, I realize that I fall far short of perfection. For example, to communicate well, I should first listen and give my full attention to the speaker. I should strive to fully understand what they are telling me, repeat what they say in my own words, and ask questions. But rather than listening, I often merely exercise patience while waiting for my children to finish so that I can talk. How hard it is to ask questions rather than to give answers!

Father, although I think I know the right answer and can compel my children to agree with me, it is better to communicate in such a way that they choose the best path.

Lord, also help me use listening skills when I come before You. Give me the patience to wait for Your message. May I tune in to You with my mind and heart.

# INTERSECTION

*How much better to get wisdom than gold,*
*to choose understanding rather than silver!*
*The highway of the upright avoids evil;*
*he who guards his way guards his life.*

PROVERBS 16:16–17 NIV

Father, my life has defining moments. At these intersections, I am presented with choices that will forever affect my family and me. Some intersections are merely different paths to the same destination. But others are clearly choices that take a measure of my character. To be a wholesome example to my children, I must choose righteousness over convenience.

Lord, You have the ability to make even my bad choices work out for me. Any incorrect decision can be righted if I will call upon Your name and repent. But I know, too, that the effect of a wrong choice can linger. It is far better to have the Christian principles and strength to make the right decision in the first place.

Father, You are at all of the intersections of my life. You are there to show me the right way to go. I pray that I'll recognize Your heavenly guidance and have the commitment to follow the correct path.

# TRUE COURSE

*Ye did run well;*
*who did hinder you that*
*ye should not obey the truth?*

GALATIANS 5:7 KJV

Dear Lord, when I am hiking with my children, I am constantly checking my direction with a compass and a trail guide. The little ones depend on me to set the right course for them. As a compass is drawn to the poles, so I am drawn to You, knowing that others follow in my steps.

Heavenly Father, my soul seeks to align in the true direction with Your mercy and grace. You, O Lord, are my righteous Creator. I pray that I will live a consecrated life through Your enabling power. Please guide me to live rightly and dispel the negative powers that could draw me off course.

Father, I pray that I will convey to my children a determination to follow the heavenly compass. May they be drawn to Your path and not depart from it.

# GRATITUDE

*Is any one of you in trouble?*
*He should pray. Is anyone happy?*
*Let him sing songs of praise.*

JAMES 5:13 NIV

Father, during a conference break, I returned to my hotel room to use the time to work on a report. As I approached, I heard singing in the room. I walked closer and discovered the maid happily doing her chores. She was singing in happiness. I listened for a moment in secret admiration and then backed away rather than disturb her.

Lord, the young woman's happiness didn't depend upon her economic condition or station in life. The song she was singing was a Christian hymn that told the source of her joy—You. Her happiness flowed naturally from the gratitude of knowing that You cared about her.

Father, I had approached the room feeling harried and stressed. But the woman showed me how to complete my day filled with gratitude and happiness. Instead of working on the report, I telephoned home and left a message assuring my children that I would be home that night in time to tuck them into bed.

# MEMORIES

*I will remember the deeds of the LORD; yes,*
*I will remember your miracles of long ago.*
*I will meditate on all your works and consider all your mighty deeds.*

PSALM 77:11–12 NIV

L ord, I've heard people who recount the events in their lives by jumping from one crisis to another. In between misfortunes, they may have experienced periods of calm or even happiness. But to them, those times are merely blank pages in their memory because they only remember those times when they were miserable.

Father, I pray that I will remember the blessings, not the trials, and enjoy happiness, not wallow in the times of distress. I recognize that happiness is not increased by material wealth nor destroyed by physical trials. Instead, it grows in proportion to how willing I am to center my heart on considering Your blessings.

Lord, I am most happy when I clearly identify what You want me to do, and I go about doing it with all my strength. Happiness as a father is leading my family in Your way and working vigorously to earn their respect and love.

# REIGN

*"And now, my children, listen to me: happy are those who keep my ways. Hear instruction and be wise, and do not neglect it."*

PROVERBS 8:32−33 NRSV

Father, I sit alone in the dim early morning light to reflect on the happiness I am feeling. I'm living a full and interesting life. I'm raising a family, luxuriating in the company of friends, and working at a job that I enjoy. As I spend time in meditation, feelings of gratitude and happiness flood over me. You have been so good to me!

Lord, I recognize You as the source of all that I possess. I express my admiration to You, the Creator, whose hand I see so clearly in every aspect of my life.

Father, may I continue to have an uninterrupted pursuit for the happiness that comes from You. I see how happy people are who put Your will before their own. I can be truly happy only as a person who yields to You. Help me reach that happy state where You reign supreme in my life.

# CHEERFUL

*I know that there is nothing better for men*
*than to be happy and do good while they live.*
*That everyone may eat and drink,*
*and find satisfaction in all his toil—this is the gift of God.*

ECCLESIASTES 3:12—13 NIV

Father, my daily life is made easier by the work of other people. I wear clothes made by strangers, some of whom live half a world away. I eat food grown on distant shores or caught in faraway oceans. I ride in vehicles assembled by hands unknown to me. I have enjoyed the labors of others.

Lord, I want to show gratitude to those who do things for me and thank those who provide personal service. Yet I see that even without personal contact, people that I have never met make my life better. I am grateful for their efforts but cannot directly repay them. But I can express my gratitude to You and show happiness to others. I can maintain an optimistic outlook and be kind and cheerful. May I increase the pool of goodwill around me by my happiness and gratitude. Help me instill in my children the spiritual fruit of joy.

## SERENITY

*"Who of you by worrying can add a single hour to his life?"*
MATTHEW 6:27 NIV

Father, thanks for calming my agitation in times of distress. With Your peace, I smile at my past foolish concerns. Some situations had already passed and could not be changed, others were unlikely to have happened, and some were trivial and not worth my emotional energy. But worry gave a small concern a long shadow. Through my actions, I could have changed only a few of the situations that troubled me.

Lord, plant me in faith, hope, and love. Shower on me the blessings that saturate my heart so thoroughly that I have room only for sensible concerns—those over which I can make a difference. I pray that I will see my troubles more clearly in Your wisdom.

Father, help me develop the serenity that produces a calming influence on others, especially the members of my family. By trusting in Your guidance, we can overcome any crisis.

# CHANGE

*For the grace of God. . .teaches us to say "No" to ungodliness
and worldly passions, and to live self-controlled, upright and godly lives
in this present age, while we wait for the blessed hope—the glorious
appearing of our great God and Savior, Jesus Christ.*

TITUS 2:11–13 NIV

Father, I tear pages from my desk calendar and see how quickly time is getting away from me. My life is in a headlong rush into a future filled with changes. I appreciate that in these changing times, You do not change. You eliminate the dread of change and fill me with hope so that I can look forward with confidence.

Lord, I pray that I develop the trust in You that brings stability to my family. Grow in us the faith to see that no matter how things turn out, problems that tax us today will be for our best in Your eternal plan. May we look beyond the dark events of today to the bright future of a home with You.

Father, I do not know what changes will overtake me in the future, but I know that You can take care of the things that concern me today and protect me from what comes against me tomorrow. You bring hope to me.

# NEVER WITHOUT

*In you I trust, O my God. Do not let me be put to shame,*
*nor let my enemies triumph over me.*
*No one whose hope is in you will ever be put to shame.*

PSALM 25:2–3 NIV

Father, sometimes I can see that my children have become despondent. Their outlook becomes gloomy. It is as if some of the light has gone out in their lives. Yet such a feeling is only justified if they are without hope. That certainly is not the case. Those who place their trust in You should never lose hope. Guide me in helping my teenage children learn ways to overcome negative emotions.

Lord, I, too, can have a troubled mind. However, I know that Your love, the grace of Jesus Christ, and the guidance of the Holy Spirit are with me. Help me face the challenges before me with boldness. Give me strength to shake off anything that troubles my mind so that I press on each day with a clear purpose. Help me ignore those troubling concerns that might slow my steps.

## CRISIS

*For he will hide me in his shelter in the day of trouble;*
*he will conceal me under the cover of his tent;*
*he will set me high on a rock.*

PSALM 27:5 NRSV

Lord, sometimes when a crisis comes my way, I am undaunted because I have faced the same problem before, and think I can handle it. But should the crisis be in an area of which I have no experience or ability, then I am plunged into despair. Most troubling are unexpected medical emergencies that strike my family. I am presented with a situation that is beyond my ability to make better. In my helplessness, I imagine the most ominous outcome. I can't think; I can't eat; I walk around as one in a daze.

Father, You are my greatest resource when a crisis strikes. I must remember that I can call upon You. Help me trust in You to carry me through the adversity. Comfort and encourage me during these difficult times. Should I ever fall into a period of depression and find it difficult to feel optimistic about the future, lift me up and let me see the bright glow of Your love.

## SHARE

*I have no greater joy than this,*
*to hear that my children are walking in the truth.*

3 JOHN 1:4 NRSV

Father, my elementary school child came home today all smiles because his teacher stamped a happy face on his class work. The happy face stamp energized his spirit, and he could not wait to share his joy with me. He had a spring in his step, and he willingly tackled more difficult homework.

Lord, my joy is not always at the full-tank level. I am sometimes at low ebb. Yet when I think about Your many blessings, it is as if You have stamped a happy face on my life.

Father, like my son, when I am filled with delight I must share it with someone else. Sharing my joy with others does not divide it but instead multiplies it. Allow me to find ways to express my joy by serving others. Equip me with the ability to spark in others the recognition that You love them.

## PROMISE

*"I have set my rainbow in the clouds,
and it will be the sign of the covenant between me and the earth.
Whenever I bring clouds over the earth and the rainbow appears
in the clouds, I will remember my covenant between me and you
and all living creatures of every kind."*

GENESIS 9:13–15 NIV

Father, when we have a storm during the daytime, I always look for a rainbow. I know one should be in the sky opposite the sun. I help my children find the rainbow and tell them the story of how You put it in the sky.

Lord, seeing a rainbow gives me joy. I am reminded how Noah and his family were saved from destruction because of Noah's obedience to You. Give me wisdom to guide my family to the ark of safety.

Father, thank You for giving all the world a visible sign of Your covenant that stretches across the heavens after a rain. All people can see and know that You keep Your promises. I pray that every time my children see a rainbow they will rejoice and be reassured that their Creator loves them and cares for them.

# SUNRISE

*Therefore my heart is glad, and my glory rejoiceth:*
*my flesh also shall rest in hope.*

PSALM 16:9 KJV

Heavenly Father, during my morning drive to work, the day is brighter and the air is cleaner than it was when I drove home the night before. Each sunrise brings a fresh day in my spiritual life, too.

Lord, seeing that each day gives me a fresh start fills me with joy. My life bubbles over with the wonderful things You have done for my family and me. I pray that my obvious and honest happiness at being a child of Yours will be apparent to my coworkers, my friends, and my family. May they also experience the joy of being Your children.

Thank You, Lord, for releasing me from my past failures so that I can face the day with a glad heart, secure in the knowledge that Jesus has given me a new start. As I drive on to my destination during the morning rush, my desire is also to stay on the spiritual highway toward my eventual destination with You.

# WARMTH

*The angel said to them, "Do not be afraid;*
*for see—I am bringing you good news of great joy for all the people:*
*to you is born this day in the city of David a Savior,*
*who is the Messiah, the Lord."*

LUKE 2:10−11 NRSV

Father, when I think about the fun of the winter holidays—with all the candles, candy, carols, and gifts—the weather doesn't seem as cold. And the bother of shoveling snow disappears when I watch my children make snow angels. The coldest season is in some ways the warmest one. It is difficult for me to give a person a cold shoulder when I hear the sounds of "Joy to the World."

Lord, I want my children to enjoy the winter holidays. I pray they will be aware of the reason we observe the birth of Your Son. Truly, He is the reason for the joy of the season.

Father, during the winter months, let me be friendly and bring warmth in opposition to the freezing weather outside. May I greet strangers with a smile so sunny that it makes them feel less need for a heavy coat.

# Guide

*By day the LORD commands his steadfast love,*
*and at night his song is with me, a prayer to the God of my life.*

Psalm 42:8 nrsv

Father, I once had a supervisor who had an open-door policy. Whenever I was torn about the best course of action for solving a problem, I would spend a few minutes talking with him. Sometimes he suggested a choice I should take or cautioned me against an option I had proposed.

Lord, I pray that my children recognize that I am willing to talk about their problems. Let them come to me so I can offer guidance. Grant me the ability to provide sensible suggestions and to correctly identify what they should do based on Your unfailing wisdom.

Father, I am thankful that You have an open-door policy. I can talk to You day or night about the things that are troubling me. It is a comfort to know that You are there to listen. I know that You will make clear to me the correct decision.

# URGENT

*Then little children were brought to Jesus for him to place his hands on them and pray for them. But the disciples rebuked those who brought them. Jesus said, "Let the little children come to me, and do not hinder them, for the kingdom of heaven belongs to such as these."*

MATTHEW 19:13–14 NIV

Father, during my busy schedule, I can see unimportant items as urgent while vital ones are shoved to the back of my mind. Answering a ringing telephone may seem urgent, but listening to my daughter tell about her day at school may be more important.

Lord, thank You for Your example of how to identify the proper choices. You encouraged little children to spend time with You. You devoted Your time to those others would have ignored.

Father, help me reschedule my time to put the important things first. The time that I spend with You and my family should take precedence over urgent matters that become meaningless after the deadline has passed.

# KNOCK

*"Here I am! I stand at the door and knock.*
*If anyone hears my voice and opens the door,*
*I will come in and eat with him, and he with me."*

REVELATION 3:20 NIV

Father, sometimes distractions can derail my train of thought. When doing paperwork at home that requires my full attention, I used to lock the door to my office so my children would not come rushing in with the latest stories of school or events on the playing field. They knocked and waited—sometimes with more patience than I thought they were capable of—until I found a stopping place and opened the door.

Once, I came by and saw my boy sitting down outside the door. The door had been closed, and he thought I was inside. He had knocked, but when he heard no answer, he sat down by the door and waited for me to come out. Now I've decided to delay work that requires quiet time until after my children go to sleep.

Father, sometimes I close the door to You, and You knock and knock in vain at my heart. But now I've decided to keep an open door to my children and to You.

# FRIENDS

*"Is there anyone among you who, if your child asks for bread,
will give a stone? Or if the child asks for a fish, will give a snake?
If you then, who are evil, know how to give good gifts to your children,
how much more will your Father in heaven give good things
to those who ask him!"*

MATTHEW 7:9–11 NRSV

Father, when I meet a friend, I take the time to ask about his day and talk with him. When he is visiting me at home, I make him comfortable, offer refreshments, and discuss subjects of interest to him. Should he have a task that needs done, I am willing to offer a helping hand. My best friend is a person who I know and trust. I know his faults, and he knows mine, but we ignore them anyway. We view one another in the best light.

Lord, I am aware that I am often more considerate of my friends than I am of members of my own family. When I seek to please everyone else at the expense of my family, I know the emphasis is in the wrong place. I should rather gain the good opinion of my family than impress any friend. Help me to treat my family with respect, dignity, and consideration.

# EMULATE

*Show yourself in all respects a model of good works,*
*and in your teaching show integrity, gravity,*
*and sound speech that cannot be censured;*
*then any opponent will be put to shame,*
*having nothing evil to say of us.*

TITUS 2:7−8 NRSV

Lord, I know that for my young children, I am a role model of You. How I treat them will shape how they will perceive You as they grow older. Will they see You as fair, affectionate, compassionate, and patient? Or will they see a father as unreasonable, aloof, callous, and impatient? Will they view You as One who provides for their needs and understands their fears? Or will they see a father as neglectful and uncaring?

Father, I want my children to approach me as one who will help. I do not want them to mistrust me. If their childhood is poisoned by fear, they may find it more difficult to approach You. If they are suspicious of my goodness, they may be unable to clearly see Your goodness. Father, I cannot perfectly emulate You, but I pray that my children see enough of You in me that they grow into an understanding of Your true, loving nature.

# APPRECIATE

*Know therefore that the LORD thy God, he is God, the faithful God,
which keepeth covenant and mercy with them that love him
and keep his commandments to a thousand generations.*

DEUTERONOMY 7:9 KJV

Omnipotent Father, there are no limitations to the
amount of love and attention You can individually
bestow upon each of Your children. Although I receive
Your rich blessings all the time, day and night, I pray that I do not
take Your love for granted.

Lord, the more I know You and understand You, the more I
see and appreciate Your love. I pray that I will experience You more
deeply so that my love for You will increase. You have taught me
that sacrifices must be made for love to grow. I submit to You.
Demolish me and then rebuild me so I may be one with You.

Father, my children are often not fully
aware of the many measures I take
to improve their lives. Although
they know they are loved, the
depth of that love is difficult
for them to comprehend.

Lord, I realize that Your
love extends beyond anything
I can comprehend.

# ACTIVE

*And so we know and rely on the love God has for us. God is love.*
*Whoever lives in love lives in God, and God in him.*

1 JOHN 4:16 NIV

Lord, I've seen parents who love a child deeply, but it is not entirely clear that the child returns that love to any depth. The lack of reciprocated love is devastating for the parents and disastrous for the child. I pray that I am not like one of those children who fails to see the love that You lavish upon me.

Father, I read that You are love. Although *love* is a small word, it stands for a concept that is too great for me to completely wrap my limited mind around. In Your goodness, You created the universe and everything in it as a place to show Your love. Develop in me the willingness to act according to Your will, not because of Your commands but because of my love for You.

Heavenly Father, I want to love You, my wife, my children, and my neighbors. Help me go beyond the emotion of love to the action of love.

# REUNION

*But if we walk in the light, as he is in the light,*
*we have fellowship with one another,*
*and the blood of Jesus, his Son, purifies us from all sin.*

1 JOHN 1:7 NIV

Father, winter holiday seasons are a time for family reunions. Now that my children are grown, married, and have children, this is my favorite time of year. Warmth radiates from hugs, smiles, and love. Grandchildren bring gifts that they have made with their own hands, and we cherish these gifts because of their special efforts.

Lord, despite our family being separated for most of the year, we hold one another in enormous respect and affection. Some people may wonder how a family that lives so far from one another can be so close. It is because we have learned the blessings of putting our lives in Your hands. All of the prayers, correction, and training that my wife and I heaped on our children when they were little have now reaped the benefit of lives living in harmony with You and fellowship with one another. Thank You for giving me this loving family.

# ARMOR

*Finally, be strong in the Lord and in his mighty power.*
*Put on the full armor of God.*

EPHESIANS 6:10–11 NIV

F ather, when I pack for a long vacation with my family, I double-check my list to be certain that we have not left anything behind. During our travels, I always take a head count before we leave a location so that no one is missing. Even the best of families can have a frightening and embarrassing situation of a child left behind.

Lord, I am also taking my family on a spiritual journey. It is important that I help them pack for that trip, as well. I need to equip them with Your armor—truth, righteousness, the good news of Jesus, faith, salvation, and the sword of the Spirit.

Father, I often become too concerned with the mundane aspects of my children's lives—clothes, sports, money, and school. I pray that I go beyond my checklists of everyday matters to the more important spiritual subjects. I pray that they are traveling with You as we journey along the road of life.

# PEER PRESSURE

*My child, keep your father's commandment, and do not forsake your mother's teaching. Bind them upon your heart always; tie them around your neck. When you walk, they will lead you; when you lie down, they will watch over you; and when you awake, they will talk with you.*

PROVERBS 6:20–22 NRSV

Heavenly Father, as my children become older, they become subject to greater peer pressure that can lead to harmful dependencies, destructive relationships, and risky behaviors. They feel pressure in countless ways—from their choices in clothing and music, to the dangers of drugs, alcohol, and immorality.

Lord, I do want to give them the freedom to make the ordinary choices of daily life. The more they trust themselves and their ability to make independent decisions, the more likely they'll be able to withstand the undue influence of peer pressure.

When my children face big decisions, give me the confidence to teach the principles from the Bible that have stood the test of time. Remind me to always be ready to give guidance based on Your Word.

# SERVE GOD

*Now therefore put away, said he, the strange gods which are among you, and incline your heart unto the LORD God of Israel. And the people said unto Joshua, The LORD our God will we serve, and his voice will we obey.*

JOSHUA 24: 23–24 KJV

Father, help me be mindful that I represent You to those I meet each day. I cannot place my Christian service in one compartment and my secular duties in another. I recall a decision faced by a friend, a real estate salesman. His supervisor told him, "Tell the truth as long as you can and then start selling." He chose to leave that employer rather than compromise his Christian principles. I admire him, and I pray that I will also be willing to suffer loss rather than discredit You.

Lord, I know that some people enjoy their jobs. Others work because they enjoy what their wages will enable them to do. But I've seen people in jobs that test their ability to remain faithful. I would not want my children to fall into such a difficult situation. I pray that through prayer and study, they will find occupations that suit their skills, interest, and abilities. Help them put being Your servants as the chief goal of their résumés.

# VOTE

*If my people, which are called by my name, shall humble themselves,*
*and pray, and seek my face, and turn from their wicked ways;*
*then will I hear from heaven, and will forgive their sin,*
*and will heal their land.*

2 CHRONICLES 7:14 KJV

Father, at each election, I cast my ballot and wear the sticker that says, "I voted." When I think about my Christian service, I realize that my most influential vote is the way that I live. Each day I make choices—the products I buy, the programs I decide to view while surfing television channels, and my willingness to participate in church activities. I vote by my attitudes and actions.

Lord, my young children may have only a slight recognition of who I voted for in an election, but every day they see if I am a moral leader and a sincere Christian. Direct me in showing them that the most important vote is how I live my life.

I pray I will vote for justice, honesty, and moral responsibility, not only at the ballot box, but also in the daily choices that I make. I want my spiritual influence to have a positive effect on my family and community.

# COUNTERFEIT

*But lay up for yourselves treasures in heaven, where neither moth nor rust doth corrupt, and where thieves do not break through nor steal.*

MATTHEW 6:20 KJV

Lord, choices come to me in pairs. Do I desire power or respect, wealth or grace, status or Your glory? Which is more important to me—worldly honor or everlasting glory, a long life on Earth or an eternal life with You? Ambition may blind me to seek a choice that will lead me away from a life of service to You.

Father, when I think about power, wealth, or status, I must ask myself where my treasures lie. Help me reject the counterfeit goals as nothing to be esteemed. I want to reject the wrong choices to make room for the right ones. May I have a genuine determination to bring Your Word into action in my life and the lives of my family. Parents can encourage their children for good or for evil. May I show them the course by word and example—that leads to the right choices.

# NOURISH

*"Yet he has not left himself without testimony: He has shown kindness
by giving you rain from heaven and crops in their seasons;
he provides you with plenty of food and fills your hearts with joy."*

ACTS 14:17 NIV

Father, I looked out this morning to see a steady, soaking
rain. I thought of my parched yard and how much the grass
needed the precipitation. Within a few minutes, the blades
of grass appeared green and glistened with life. Everything appears
brighter and healthier after the rain.

Help me keep in mind, Lord, that it is my duty to nourish my
children in all aspects of their lives. Lord, sometimes we become
spiritually dry. Like a drought, the condition creeps in slowly over
time. But Your Word refreshes our souls, strengthens us, and gives
us spiritual growth.

Lord, help me constantly monitor the
spiritual condition of my children
and myself. Before our strength
grows weak, please send heavenly water to refresh our souls
and rejuvenate our worship. I
pray that Your abundant blessings will continue to fall on my
family and me.

# GROWTH

*Then he said to his disciples,*
*"The harvest is plentiful, but the laborers are few;*
*therefore ask the Lord of the harvest to send out laborers into his harvest."*
MATTHEW 9:37–38 NRSV

Father, even from my limited gardening experience, I've seen that weeds grow without encouragement, but good crops require attention. Seeds must be planted in soil that has been prepared to receive them, the weeds must be eliminated, and the produce must be harvested at the right time.

Almighty Savior, I see that the same sequence is necessary to produce a harvest in the spiritual domain. Pull my sin out by the roots, and spiritually refresh me with the water of life.

Lord, as I embark upon the stage of my life as a father, I pray that I will be wise in ensuring that my children grow strong in Your love. Help me to be diligent in the work that brings my children to You. Lord, make me a faithful worker in Your harvest. May I have an urgency to gather them into Your kingdom before the season is past and Your crop is lost.

# VITAMINS

*My people are destroyed for lack of knowledge.*

HOSEA 4:6 KJV

Heavenly Father, my doctor told me a dietary deficiency was causing the skin to flake from my fingers. Despite healthy meals, some essential component was missing from my diet. The doctor recommended a minor change to what I ate, and the problem disappeared.

Father, if I search through Your Word and read only those passages that I find agreeable to my preconceived ideas of Your message, then I am missing some of the essential elements that I need for a strong relationship with You. I pray that I choose to become healthy by accepting all the spiritual vitamins that You have provided for me.

Lord, some diseases are not obvious to the eyes alone. As children grow to become young adults, they may have healthy bodies, but tragically, their lives are in turmoil because they have made wrong spiritual decisions. Please help me take care to nourish my children's lives with the full sustenance of the good news of Jesus.

# INDEPENDENCE

*"Then you will know the truth, and the truth will set you free."*

JOHN 8:32 NIV

Heavenly Father, summer travel brochures always show a person on vacation strolling along a white sand beach, lying in a hammock, or watching a sunset. My vacations aren't as leisurely, and before they are over I look forward to returning to work. Independence Day is my favorite summer holiday because it has the good sense to last only one day—backyard barbecue, ball game, evening fireworks, and then it's over.

Thank You, Lord, for my personal independence day, the day You broke me away from sin so I could begin a personal, daily relationship with You.

Father, my children are always pushing for greater independence, and I do give them freedom that promotes growth. Because of the grounding that they have in faith, I am confident they are growing spiritually, too. May they see their growing independence as a reason to base more of their lives in obedience that brings them closer to You.

# BOUNDARIES

*Children, obey your parents in everything,*
*for this is your acceptable duty in the Lord.*
*Fathers, do not provoke your children, or they may lose heart.*

COLOSSIANS 3:20—21 NRSV

Father, as I watch my young daughter coloring a picture, I see her tongue at the corner of her mouth and her face in deep concentration. She is determined not to go outside the lines. Finally, she manages to finish in triumph. I take it to hang in my office.

Lord, I am working to provide my daughter an environment that has reasonable boundaries and guidelines. If she works as hard staying within those boundaries as she does staying inside the lines of her coloring book, then she will be successful. But it took dozens of drawings before she succeeded at her coloring. I pray that I recognize her efforts to improve.

Father, I have not been able to control my life perfectly. Thank You for helping me get back within the boundaries You have set for me. May I be as patient with my children as You have been with me.

## COMPLIANCE

*But the steadfast love of the LORD is from everlasting to everlasting*
*on those who fear him, and his righteousness to children's children,*
*to those who keep his covenant and remember to do his commandments.*

PSALM 103:17–18 NRSV

Father, when it is time for my children to leave a playground, I give the final call and start for the car. They come, but at a snail's pace. They drag their feet and divert from one piece of playground equipment along their path to the next. They pretend they are obeying my call, but their actions show otherwise. I explain to them that delay or an excessively slow response is not obedience.

Lord, how many times have You seen my obedience in this way? I say I will do something, but I find ways to put it off or accomplish it a piece at a time without giving it my earnest effort.

Father, children who do not listen to their parents often end up in difficult circumstances. Yet I sometimes find myself being as deaf to Your commands as my children are to mine. Please forgive my slow response and childish attempts to avoid the work You have given me.

# ENTHUSIASM

*For by thee I have run through a troop:*
*by my God have I leaped over a wall.*

2 SAMUEL 22:30 KJV

Father, I wish to develop a trusting acceptance of Your will. Grant me the willingness to accept Your plans for me with obedient enthusiasm.

Lord, I recognize the need for a strong faith, but may I never try to impose my human will on Your sovereign power. Sometimes I come before You in prayer with an agenda of things that I think needs done. I look at the list and toss it aside. What do I know about Your intention for my life? It is not my demands that need addressed but Your will. Grant me the willingness to trust and accept Your purpose.

Father, You still have faith in me after all the times that I have failed to show a strong faith in You. I pray that I continue to grow in faith and shape my life according to Your will. May my family see that not only do I have faith but also that I shape my life by it.

# LEARNING

*The seed is the word of God. But that on the good ground are they,*
*which in an honest and good heart, having heard the word, keep it,*
*and bring forth fruit with patience.*

LUKE 8:11, 15 KJV

Father, my son was supposed to wait for the carpool to hockey practice, but when they called to say they would be late, he decided to ride his bike. He carried his hockey stick across the handlebars. He took a tumble when the stick caught on a sign. Later, I asked what had caused the accident. He thought for a moment and gave the correct answer—impatience.

Lord, like my son, I often lack patience. I can usually trace lost opportunities and troubles to being impatient. Often, the object that gains my attention and to which I run is not important enough to justify the effort.

Father, help me reschedule my life so I can let go of the lesser things. May I seize the important values that should rule my life. I am thankful that You see my impatient mistakes—and help me out of them. You help me grow into a stronger, more patient person.

# SPECIAL

*Finally, brothers, whatever is true, whatever is noble, whatever is right,*
*whatever is pure, whatever is lovely, whatever is admirable—*
*if anything is excellent or praiseworthy—think about such things.*

PHILIPPIANS 4:8 NIV

Father, I took my family on a glass-bottom boat tour of coral reefs. The tour guide told us that it took many years for tiny organisms to develop the colorful coral reefs that we could view through the underwater windows.

Lord, thank You for Your creation. Some things I can readily see, but others are hidden from ordinary vision. As I look at other people, direct me to realize that I cannot always see the work You are doing in their lives. Give me patience to look for the things that are good in others.

Father, I know that Your creative power is still shaping individuals to become more like You. Like the coral reef that is difficult to see under the ocean's surface, desirable qualities are sometimes difficult to see in others. Take away from me any judgmental spirit. Adjust my thoughts and the thoughts of my children to think on the worth You have placed on each individual person.

# WILLPOWER

*For bodily exercise profiteth little:*
*but godliness is profitable unto all things,*
*having promise of the life that now is, and of that which is to come.*

1 TIMOTHY 4:8 KJV

Father, along with getting older has come an expanding waistline. Controlling my weight is a constant challenge. I exercise regularly and am selective of the foods I eat, but maintaining a healthy weight is still a problem. The Bible reassures us that You are not as concerned with our outward appearance as You are with the condition of our hearts.

Lord, help me to direct my children to feast on the spiritual food of Your Word. Give them the willpower to overcome evil and temptations that would weaken their witness for You. As my children grow into adulthood, develop in them the characteristics that will make them beautiful for You.

Father, help me pursue these worthy goals knowing that I do not achieve them by brief effort but by lifelong commitment to a righteous course of action. Lord, my prayer is that daily You will transform me to live a life that will bring honor to You.

## SACRIFICE

*For our light affliction, which is but for a moment,*
*worketh for us a far more exceeding and eternal weight of glory.*

2 CORINTHIANS 4:17 KJV

Father, I must visit the dentist far more often now because I avoided dental care in my early years. When I was younger, I put off as long as possible what I hoped I could get out of doing altogether. But a few minutes of discomfort in the dentist's chair back then would have guarded against hours of toothache today. I chose to avoid the dentist, and now I pay the price.

Lord, I am thankful that this distressing pattern has not developed in my children. Whether it's from my negative example or better character traits acquired from their mother, my children appear to be following a better way.

Lord, help me exercise good judgment to accept the sacrifice that it takes to be a true Christian. I know that my efforts are minor compared to the rewards that await me in the future life.

# CONTROLLED

*"Then you will call upon me and come and pray to me,*
*and I will listen to you.*
*You will seek me and find me when you seek me with all your heart."*

JEREMIAH 29:12–13 NIV

Father, I have a friend, an airplane pilot, who has an instrument flight rating. When dark clouds surround him, when all visual contact with the ground is lost, he continues on by relying on the airplane's instruments and the directions given by air traffic controllers. He has been trained not merely to read the instruments but to trust them even when he becomes disoriented.

Lord, sometime the troubles of this world surround me. I become spiritually disoriented. To avoid disaster, I must direct my course by talking to You in prayer and accepting Your Word as the guide to get me through the dark times.

Father, my children have come to me tilted from their equilibrium by the conflicting messages of the world. Direct me in how to point them to You as the Master of their lives. They will stay on course only by putting themselves under the control of Your higher authority.

# AUTHENTIC

*I do not cease to give thanks for you as I remember you in my prayers.*
*I pray that the God of our Lord Jesus Christ, the Father of glory,*
*may give you a spirit of wisdom and revelation as you come to know him.*

EPHESIANS 1:16–17 NRSV

Father, I face many challenges in my Christian walk. These challenges can be overcome with prayers that specifically address what is troubling me. Often, my prayers fail because I sink into a rote pattern. I am merely mouthing words but do not take up the authentic issues at the core of my concern. I do not address what is, or should be, on my heart.

Lord, when I read Your Word, I find prayers by the heroes of faith—Moses, Joshua, David, Peter, Paul, and many others. They prayed for wisdom, confidence, guidance, boldness, restoration, healing, and safekeeping. They prayed during a time of crisis, and their prayers went to the heart of the matter.

Father, I seek Your blessings in the practical, day-to-day issues of my life—my joys, fears, and aspirations. I pray that I will study Your Word so that it serves as a launching point into a deeper, more forceful prayer time.

# HEAVEN'S GATE

*Keep yourselves in the love of God, looking for the mercy of our Lord
Jesus Christ unto eternal life.*

JUDE 21 KJV

Father, after I became an adult, my father influenced me
more than any other person in my life. As his life drew to
a close, we knew that he would soon leave this world for a
better one. I remember an airplane flight that mirrored my feelings.
As the airplane descended into clouds for landing, the ride became
bumpy. The plane shook as the lashing rain buffeted it. But after
we dipped below the clouds and touched down, the setting sun
illuminated everything with a warm glow. At the gate, my family
welcomed me home.

Lord, like the airplane flight, a few bumps have reminded me of
how blessed the rest of my life has been. When I arrive at my final
destination, I will be illuminated by Your light. Those who have
gone before me, including my mother
and father, will be there welcoming me
home. Lord, help me prepare for living
at home forever with You.

# BLESSINGS

*"Stand up and praise the LORD your God,*
*who is from everlasting to everlasting."*
*"Blessed be your glorious name,*
*and may it be exalted above all blessing and praise."*

NEHEMIAH 9:5 NIV

Father, I come to spend some time with You in conversation. Today, I wish to express my thanks for all You have done for me. You have provided me with a loving family, and we have enjoyed Your protection and blessings.

Lord, I know that all good things come from You. Sometimes I think only of the things I have as indications of blessings. I am guilty of looking with the green eyes of envy at others who appear to have received richer portions. But often when their situation is fully revealed, I have no desire to trade any part of my life with them. Open my eyes to see that the things I do not have would be detrimental to my relationship with You.

Father, I pray that I can always express my love for You and my thankfulness for Your blessings in my life.

# SAFETY

*"Because of the oppression of the weak and the groaning of the needy,
I will now arise," says the LORD. "I will protect them from those
who malign them." And the words of the LORD are flawless,
like silver refined in a furnace of clay, purified seven times. O LORD,
you will keep us safe and protect us from such people forever.*

PSALM 12:5−7 NIV

Lord, raising a family is a daunting task. Just as I learn what is required for children at a certain age, they grow older, and an entirely different set of skills is needed. But in all stages of their lives, I must offer my children patience, understanding, wisdom, and protection. Equip me in abundance with the characteristics I need to provide for them and keep them safe. I ask for Your constant help and boundless compassion.

Father, I see my role as a shepherd. Not only must I lead my family in the right direction, I must also protect them from the evil that will attempt to snatch them away. I want my children to have a loving home that is a place of safety where they are always welcome.

# GUARDIAN

*Behold, the angel of the Lord appeareth to Joseph in a dream, saying,*
*Arise, and take the young child and his mother, and flee into Egypt,*
*and be thou there until I bring thee word: for Herod will seek the young*
*child to destroy him. When he arose, he took the young child and*
*his mother by night, and departed into Egypt.*

MATTHEW 2:13–14 KJV

Father, I know of children who have been placed in the care of a guardian. I admire men who can step in and take over the duties of a father to children who do not biologically belong to them. In many cases, the father has missed the formative years in which the child is most easily molded. An adopted or foster child has added emotional baggage because of frequent moves and unstable situations. Acting as an adoptive or foster father is an enormous task!

Lord, I think of Joseph, who took on the role of being the father of Jesus. Because of the threats to the newborn baby, Joseph willingly uprooted his family and escaped to a distant country.

Father, I pray that I am willing to make the sacrifices to ensure that my family is protected from the evil in this world.

# EXAGGERATION

*I have seen all the works that are done under the sun; and,
behold, all is vanity and vexation of spirit.*

ECCLESIASTES 1:14 KJV

Father, each day I am bombarded with advertisements. I am assured that the merchandise is on the leading edge. I suddenly discover a product is essential although I have been getting along without it all of my life. I disparage as outdated my perfectly serviceable possessions.

Lord, advertisements target each one of my family members regardless of our ages. I am concerned that my younger children may believe that eating a certain cereal will give them amazing physical powers. I cringe as glamorous fashion models assure my older daughter that a certain shampoo will change her life. Help me protect them from these exaggerated claims.

Heavenly Father, I pray that my family and I will not allow advertisements to encourage our tendency to be discontent. Help us dismiss sales pitches that appeal to desire and pride. Keep us away from the idea that we can improve our future with things rather than living right for You.

# VALUES

*The simple believeth every word:*
*but the prudent man looketh well to his going.*

PROVERBS 14:15 KJV

Lord, every day my eyes and ears are beset with those who want to bend my will to their purposes. Testimonies from famous personalities, glittering television advertisements, and half-truths of insincere politicians are all trying to muddle my reasoning so I cannot distinguish between truth and lies. They want us to listen and not ask questions. I try to protect my children from the glitzy advertising and forceful efforts that assail their eyes and ears.

I am well aware that many advertisers attack a person's basic convictions with persuasive arguments in order to substitute alternate beliefs. My children come under the influence of those who attempt to program their minds. Father, help me use the abilities You have given me to carefully evaluate the claims made by those who are trying to influence me. Help me teach my children to use all the abilities You have given them to separate the false from the true.

# GIVING

*The plans of the diligent lead to profit
as surely as haste leads to poverty.*

PROVERBS 21:5 NIV

Father, with the start of each new school year, I can look forward to my school-age children being involved in a variety of fund-raising projects. They range from offering to do yard work, to the walks for this or that cause, to the selling of nutrition-questionable boxes of candy.

Lord, it seems every cause has a compelling reason why I should support the effort. I find it difficult to separate the vital few from the trivial many. I cannot learn enough about every group's programs to fully support what they are doing. Give me the wisdom to direct my support to those who are carrying out Your will. I pray I will always be willing to make sacrifices, but keep me from being a wasteful giver.

Heavenly Father, You have abundantly blessed me. Guide me to practical ways that I can be a benefit to those who are doing Your will.

# WEALTH

*Let your conversation be without covetousness;*
*and be content with such things as ye have: for he hath said,*
*I will never leave thee, nor forsake thee.*

HEBREWS 13:5 KJV

Dear Lord, You know I worry about money. Not because I am afraid I will not have enough, but because of my concern for those who depend upon me. I feel a strong obligation to provide for my family.

Father, help me understand the joy of honest effort and the emptiness of gain by dishonest means. Remind me that piling up wealth for wealth alone casts a gloomy shadow over a person's life. May I realize that what I do have far exceeds what I do not have. I pray for abundance of the heart and not of possession.

Lord, prevent me from using my role as a provider to rationalize an excessive devotion to making money. I pray that I will never measure success by material wealth or possessions or think of money as a symbol of my virility. Thank You for assuring me that You will fulfill the needs of my family.

# JUST IN TIME

*Now he who supplies seed to the sower and bread for food will also*
*supply and increase your store of seed and will enlarge the harvest*
*of your righteousness. You will be made rich in every way*
*so that you can be generous on every occasion, and*
*through us your generosity will result in thanksgiving to God.*

2 CORINTHIANS 9:10—11 NIV

Father, at one time, I worked for a company that had a "just in time" inventory system. Computers tracked sales and ordered additional stock at the right moment to replenish what was needed.

Lord, I know that You are far more dependable than any system devised by humankind. But You know that I struggle to avoid needless worry, especially when it comes to events affecting my family.

All of my past experience shows me that You always grant what I need when I need it. The supply is always there at the right moment. Remind me to put aside my needless worry and instead concentrate on living with the confidence that You will provide.

# LIVING WATER

*"If anyone is thirsty, let him come to me and drink.
Whoever believes in me, as the Scripture has said,
streams of living water will flow from within him."*

JOHN 7:37–38 NIV

Father, while traveling in desert country, I was surprised to come across a group of people going scuba diving. One of the small communities had grown up around a huge natural spring. The spring's source offered a place to make deep dives in the middle of a dry climate. The constant flow of water turned nearby fields green. The spring gave life to the desert and drew travelers to it.

Lord, in the Bible, Jesus describes Himself as "living water." I trust that my family and I will always gather around the source of eternal life to refresh our spirits. You are the One who brings life to the branches.

Father, the hardest of soil can be made fertile, and the driest of grass can be made green when water is available. Help me be a refreshing example of Your living water to others.

## ENVIRONMENT

*He came out and went, as was his custom, to the Mount of Olives; and the disciples followed him. Then he withdrew from them about a stone's throw, knelt down, and prayed.*

LUKE 22:39, 41 NRSV

Father, I have a friend who has trained himself to make weather forecasts. He looks at temperature, dew point, humidity, cloud cover, and prevailing winds. He understands that each weather phenomenon is produced by a distinctive set of weather conditions. The environment must be right to give rise to a particular weather formation.

Lord, I realize that to achieve my spiritual goals, I need to ensure that my surroundings provide the proper environment. A loving, godly home can only be produced by the right conditions. I need to respect my wife, spend time with my children, be a role model and teacher, show affection, and provide an environment where my dedication to You is readily apparent.

Father, I will turn on the telephone answering machine, turn off the television and video games, and arrange our chairs so we focus on the family devotion. Grant us the good sense to schedule time with You first, before the events of the day capture our attention.

# REST

*Six days you shall do your work, but on the seventh day you shall rest,
so that your ox and your donkey may have relief,
and your homeborn slave and the resident alien may be refreshed.*

EXODUS 23:12 NRSV

Father, I am struck by how some people do not need to be encouraged to work. Instead, many must be persuaded to rest. At work, when I become involved in a challenging project or am given an interesting assignment, I often work through my break and cut short my lunchtime. Eventually, the unceasing effort can cause adverse effects, and I must relent and take a break.

Lord, I appreciate that You have given instruction to take a day of rest. I appreciate a day of study to better understand Your will, a day to focus on worship and fellowship, a day to change my heart from earthly affairs to heavenly ones. The day becomes a refreshing change.

Father, every day is Your day, but thank You for giving me a day to seek release from the workweek responsibilities and stress. Help me guide my family into activities that strengthen us and prepare us for the battles that we face during the week.

# TRANSFORM

*Our message of the gospel came to you not in word only, but also in power and in the Holy Spirit and with full conviction; just as you know what kind of persons we proved to be among you for your sake.*

1 THESSALONIANS 1:5 NRSV

Father, I confess to You that I often read the Bible hurriedly and without much comprehension. Despite my sometimes superficial reading, I always gain something from staying in touch with You. More gratifying, though, are those occasions when I take the time to think upon Your Word and meditate upon Your message. For several days I carry the verses around in my thoughts and pray about them. Slowly, by continually holding them in my mind, they dawn into full light.

Lord, reading Your Word and studying it closely renews me each day. I can see more clearly my responsibilities to You and to those around me, including my wife and children. Guide me to pursue those passages in the Bible that hold meaning for each situation I face.

Father, I pray that the power of Your Word will transform my mind. Change the printed words into words written on my heart and living in my spirit.

# STUDY

*"But those who drink of the water that I will give them will never be thirsty. The water that I will give will become in them a spring of water gushing up to eternal life."*

JOHN 4:14 NRSV

Heavenly Father, I saw a sign warning hikers going into a desert park to take water and drink it. I was surprised at the seemingly obvious second part of the warning. But park rangers have found hikers unconscious from dehydration, who were carrying full canteens! The victims had the water they needed to preserve their lives, but they failed to drink it.

Father, may I be ever mindful of the importance of constantly drinking Your living water. May my family and I always spend time reading Your Word, praying, and having daily devotions. Only in this way will we have the spiritual refreshment to meet the challenges of everyday life.

Lord Jesus, I am blessed to have so many ways to learn about Your will. The Bible says You, Lord Jesus, are the source of water that quenches spiritual thirst. Thank You for granting me the water that brings everlasting life.

# RESPECT

*Moreover, we had human parents to discipline us, and we respected them.*
*Should we not be even more willing to be subject*
*to the Father of spirits and live?*

HEBREWS 12:9 NRSV

Lord, although I do not often acknowledge it, I realize that the respect of my family is important to me. I see other men who are devastated when they lose the respect of someone they cherish. I have heard that for some fathers, being respected by their families is more important than being loved. "Not me, Lord," I say. But I know I can be shattered by a word rashly spoken, especially by my wife, or by my children when I sense that they view some aspect of my personality in less than flattering terms.

Father, I know that it is impossible to please everyone. But I do wish to be highly regarded by my family and by those whose opinions are important to me. I pray that I inspire respect by serving and by making sacrifices. Remove from me the concern that my sense of purpose depends on how others view me. Replace it with my concern with how You regard me.

## LEADERSHIP

*At Caesarea there was a man named Cornelius,
a centurion in what was known as the Italian Regiment.
He and all his family were devout and God-fearing;
he gave generously to those in need and prayed to God regularly.*

ACTS 10:1–2 NIV

Lord, sometimes I look around and see all kinds of sin in this world. I let my guard down, and I am tempted to say or do something I know is wrong. In a moment like that, I remember the account of Noah. He refused to compromise his righteous walk with You, Lord.

In the Bible, I read how the righteousness of a father influenced those around him. Cornelius, the centurion, and his entire family are described as "devout." As a father, I want to lead my whole family to You and keep them in fellowship with You.

Dear God, help me to find favor in the eyes of those around me and especially in Your eyes by maintaining Christian traits. The most important concern in my life is that my family and I will please You.

## INTEGRITY

*He kneeled upon his knees three times a day,*
*and prayed, and gave thanks before his God, as he did aforetime.*

DANIEL 6:10 KJV

Lord, I want to live an upright life no matter how difficult the circumstances. I look to Daniel as an example of one who was not afraid to do what was right, even though he faced death in a den of lions. You gave him protection and blessed his integrity.

Heavenly Father, I want to be like Daniel, who held fast to his faith despite great demands to do otherwise. His story strengthens me, and I pray that it will also strengthen my children as they mature and go out into the world. When they face tough times, I pray they will continue to put their trust in You.

O Lord, in reading about Daniel, I see how he devoted himself to prayer and thanksgiving. Give me a strong faith to share with my family. You are more powerful than any enemies of my soul, and You have every situation of my life under control.

# WONDER

*O LORD, how manifold are thy works!*
*in wisdom hast thou made them all:*
*the earth is full of thy riches.*

PSALM 104:24 KJV

Lord, Your creation provokes a sense of wonder in me. From the rocky shores with crashing surf to a humid rainforest with water dripping from the trees, the range of Your creation is beyond comprehension. I feel the same wonder when I read from Your Word. It contains wonderful poetry and soul-stirring songs. I read in it exciting stories of the heroes of faith. I marvel at miraculous events that are beyond human comprehension. Each day of reading the Bible is a new adventure and a wonderful journey. Holy scripture is a light that guides me to righteousness.

Lord, I pray that I can instill in my children a sense of wonder in Your creation and Your Word. I pray that for them and for me, Your Word will always be fresh and will illuminate our lives. I pray that we will read Your Word, contemplate Your message, and keep it in our minds throughout each day.

# PERFECTION

*Do not conform any longer to the pattern of this world,*
*but be transformed by the renewing of your mind.*
*Then you will be able to test and approve what God's will is—*
*his good, pleasing and perfect will.*

ROMANS 12:2 NIV

Father, through You, I know the qualities a good father should possess. I am thankful that I have You as a model of what I should be. Qualities like kindness, selflessness, reassurance, and attentiveness are just a few. But I know that children do not always experience the love and care that You intend for us as fathers to provide.

Lord, to have the authority to direct my household in the ways of righteousness and truth, my family must recognize me as being an example of one who does Your will. Only by my study of the Bible, frequent conversation with You, and thankfulness for Your blessings will they have confidence that I know what I am doing.

Father, guide me as I faithfully train my children. I desire to show them a consistent pattern of what it means to be a loving father. Because I cannot measure up to perfection, I pray that they will look beyond me to You.

# HERO

*For this slight momentary affliction is preparing us for an eternal weight of glory beyond all measure, because we look not at what can be seen but at what cannot be seen; for what can be seen is temporary, but what cannot be seen is eternal.*

2 CORINTHIANS 4:17−18 NRSV

Father, while working out at the gym, I've seen people wearing shirts with a professional athlete's name and jersey number. The writing shows whom they admire.

Lord, I am not an athlete, so others are unlikely to wear a shirt with my name on it. But I simply desire that the characteristics my family and others see in me will be those of a faithful Christian. Help me express to my children that earthly fame is temporary, but Christian principals are eternal.

Father, help my children become aware that the outward persona of a person may conceal a character that is not worthy of admiration. I pray that they will never become so enamored with a public figure that they are shattered when their hero is revealed to have failed. Instead, I pray that they emulate the One who never fails and acknowledge You above all others.

# INFLUENCE

*Hold to the standard of sound teaching that you have heard from me,
in the faith and love that are in Christ Jesus.
Guard the good treasure entrusted to you,
with the help of the Holy Spirit living in us.*

2 TIMOTHY 1:13−14 NRSV

Father, when in a boat, I am surprised at the strength of the waves generated by other boats. A vessel may be well away from me and pass at slow speed. The boat seems to produce a gentle swell on the water, but the waves strike my boat with a solid slapping sound that reveals their full power. The waves can continue to rock my boat long after the vessel that caused them has passed.

Lord, I understand that the way I conduct my life can also have a far-reaching influence. Consequences may only become apparent long after my efforts have ended. Father, I pray that others feel my influence and that it is a positive one. Lord, help me to communicate Your love to my children by my relationship with You and by my compassion for others. Guide me in the way of righteousness.

# WALK WITH GOD

*Noah was a righteous man,*
*blameless among the people of his time,*
*and he walked with God.*

GENESIS 6:9 NIV

Lord, I am largely defined by those whom I choose as heroes and models for my life. Others interpret my character by the characters of those with whom I walk. I want to be like the heroes of old, those men of renown in the Bible, who were described as having "walked with God."

Dear Father, give me the determination to walk at Your side. I seek an honorable walk that shows Your power and character. I know that I am not walking alone; You are with me. I have the victory over impossible circumstances because I have placed myself in Your footsteps.

Father, I pray, too, that my children recognize that their choices of friends will profoundly affect their lives. Help me provide them the opportunity to develop friendships with those who share the vision to be effective Christians.

# NEWBORN

*A good man leaves an inheritance for his children's children.*

PROVERBS 13:22 NIV

Eight pounds and eight ounces, twenty-one inches long. As I hold my newborn son and watch him sleep in peace, I cannot help but wonder what the future holds. A lot is expected of me—and of him. He will carry my name and represent me in extending my hopes beyond what I have accomplished. Lord, it is humbling to realize that You have given me still another little life. I accept the responsibility to provide for him and train his body and mind. I pray for Your guidance in this awesome responsibility.

Dear Lord, I pray I will give him the freedom to find his own way, but also ground him in the essentials of Your Word. I pray that he inherits from me a name that he will be pleased to wear. But more than anything, I pray that beside my name in the Book of Life, I will see his name also written there.

# FATHER

*I will meditate on all your works and consider all your mighty deeds.*

PSALM 77:12 NIV

Father, my little boy stands at the window and waves good-bye each morning as I leave for work. He does not wonder what I do all day. To him, my only job is being his father. I have a routine job and my position in the company is nothing out of the ordinary. But if I were the president of a large corporation or a part-time employee of a small company, it would not matter to him. My business is to be his father, and that is all he cares to know at this age.

Father, in my relationship with You, I am often like the self-centered little boy. I should comprehend more fully the vast work that You do. As my child matures, he will become more aware of the many responsibilities that I carry and the many unseen tasks that I do for him. I pray, too, that as I gain wisdom and understanding, I will appreciate the multiple actions that You do for me each day.

# TEEN

*A prudent man sees danger and takes refuge, but the simple keep going
and suffer for it. Humility and the fear of the LORD bring wealth and
honor and life. In the paths of the wicked lie thorns and snares,
but he who guards his soul stays far from them.*

PROVERBS 22:3–5 NIV

Father, I pray for my son. He has begun the turbulent teen
years. I renew my determination to be a father who is present in his life. I know that a boy in a home with a loving
father is far more likely to complete his education, find secure
employment, and avoid illegal activities. The dark side of the teen
years—drug abuse, sexual immorality, and suicide—are less likely to
occur if I remain engaged as a father. He, too, has made a commitment to You and that gives me comfort.

Lord, despite my efforts and his hard work, much depends
upon circumstances that are out of our hands. I cringe at the
demands that assail him by the secular
world. My only refuge is to pray that
You will protect him so that he comes
out on the other side of his teen years
strong in his walk with You.

# AIM HIGH

*And other [seed] fell on good ground, and sprang up,*
*and bare fruit an hundredfold.*
*But that on the good ground are they,*
*which in an honest and good heart, having heard the word,*
*keep it, and bring forth fruit with patience.*

LUKE 8:8, 15 KJV

Heavenly Father, my son is old enough to take a greater role in his life. The decisions he makes will both reflect his character and mold his further development. Father, I pray that my son develops worthy characteristics as he grows and matures. May he become a person devoted to honest effort. I pray that he will expend his efforts on problems worthy of attack. Should he fail, may the reason be that he aimed too high rather than that he accepted defeat too readily.

Father, I cannot ask my son to meet these goals unless I first develop them in myself and become grounded in Your teachings. I know my advice will only take root if I plant it in the soil of good example. Teach me to choose the honorable path.

# Spiritual Education

*You therefore, beloved, since you are forewarned,*
*beware that you are not carried away with the error*
*of the lawless and lose your own stability.*
*But grow in the grace and knowledge of*
*our Lord and Savior Jesus Christ.*
*To him be the glory both now and to the day of eternity. Amen.*

2 Peter 3:17–18 nrsv

Father, I am struck by the fact that despite the wealth of a great nation, citizens with an inferior education may live as if they were in an underdeveloped country. Often, I fail to understand that this principle applies to my spiritual life, as well.

Lord, my family and I are blessed with so many ways to delve deeply into Your Word. The Bible is available in both paper and electronic form. Bible dictionaries and other aids for studying scripture abound in many editions. Dedicated teachers conduct Bible studies tailored for every age group and level of expertise. I pray, dear Father, that we will take advantage of these opportunities to have a world-class spiritual education so that we eliminate the poverty of spiritual ignorance.

Heavenly Father, open my eyes to opportunities to have family devotions. I resolve to read the Bible, pray, and have a short devotion together sometime each day.

# DIRECTIONS

*All scripture is inspired by God and is useful for teaching, for reproof, for correction, and for training in righteousness, so that everyone who belongs to God may be proficient, equipped for every good work.*

2 TIMOTHY 3:16–17 NRSV

Father, I spent the morning trying to put together the barbecue grill, which was labeled, "Some assembly required." If I had read the directions to begin with, it would have been simpler—maybe. Even when I did bring myself to read the directions, I couldn't figure out what was required of me.

Lord, sometimes I try to put my life together without reading Your directions. Thank You for providing a clear set of directions for life. Thankfully, I can read Your Word and understand the principles that make me—Your creation—function correctly.

Father, I want my children to also understand the benefits of having daily guidance from Your Word. A well-read Bible in my hands is a powerful example to my children of its importance. Build our faith that You have the answers when we face life's questions. Please guide us to Your Word before we become confused by the world's ineffective counsel.

# MENTOR

*These are the things that you shall do: Speak the truth to one another, render in your gates judgments that are true and make for peace.*

ZECHARIAH 8:16 NRSV

Father, I occasionally take on the role of a teacher, although I often feel inadequate for the task. My goal is to be a mentor, guide, and advisor. May I grow in knowledge, wisdom, character, and confidence so I can help those whom I teach to choose the proper path.

Lord, as a father, I want to encourage my children to study for careers that match their abilities. I also desire for them to decide to serve You in every aspect of their lives. Give me the talent to instill in them the realization that worship of You is a daily activity that includes all aspects of their lives including their jobs.

Heavenly Teacher, provide me with the ability to instill in my children a love for learning more about You, reading the Bible, talking to You in prayer, and living a life in keeping with Your Word. May I have an influence that will last a lifetime.

# EXAMPLE

*For I have given you an example,*
*that ye should do as I have done to you.*

JOHN 13:15 KJV

Model the ideal behavior," a supervisor told me when I was taking a class to train others. "Show examples of the skill you want to transfer to the other employees, and give them guided practice." I found that neither textbook nor lecture taught as well as a real-life demonstration.

Heavenly Father, I appreciate reading about the life of Your Son and seeing how He taught the world about Your love through His examples and teaching. He portrayed compassion by healing the sick and feeding the multitudes. He expressed the depth of Your forgiveness by giving His life for my sins.

Lord, now it is time for me to model the right behavior for my family. I cannot delegate to others the lifesaving spiritual examples my children need. I need to communicate Your teachings by a wholesome life and genuine love for You. May they see my joy in serving You so that they, too, are drawn to You.

# BLESSED

*As you also join in helping us by your prayers,*
*so that many will give thanks on our behalf for the blessing*
*granted us through the prayers of many.*

2 CORINTHIANS 1:11 NRSV

Father, my life is filled with many rich blessings. I am grateful for Your Son, whose grace continually removes the blemishes of sin from my life. I appreciate the comfort of the Holy Spirit, who guides me to righteousness. I am thankful to You, O Lord, for Your unfailing love.

Lord, many people have been a blessing in my life. My mother held me and loved me when I felt no one cared. My father supported me and gave me his time, attention, and companionship. Thank You for a wife who is affectionate, considerate, and willing to help me overcome my weaknesses. Many others—relatives, friends, and coworkers—favor me each day with their kindness and consideration.

Father, I am especially thankful for my children. On special days they give me hand-drawn cards, which mean more than any expensive gift made with other hands. Because of their warm love and respect, they have a way of brightening the darkest day.

# BOUNTIFUL

*Enter into his gates with thanksgiving, and into his courts with praise:*
*be thankful unto him, and bless his name.*

PSALM 100:4 KJV

Dear Lord, what bountiful harvest I have received from You! I count blessings without number. You have given me health, prosperity, and a peaceful heart. You have given me strength in adversity and security in turmoil. You have shown me opportunities to serve and have thereby enriched my life.

Father, I am thankful for a warm family life. My wife adds a marvelous sparkle to each day. My children keep my body active and my mind sharp. Most of all, I am thankful that we receive the bountiful benefit of Your love.

Lord, I acknowledge in this prayer of thanksgiving the rich blessings that have fallen on me. Help me appreciate them. Keep from my mind the thought that I am entitled to them because of anything I have done. Let me focus on what You have done and rejoice in all Your daily blessings.

# HIDDEN

*The eye cannot say to the hand, "I don't need you!" And the head cannot say to the feet, "I don't need you!"*

1 CORINTHIANS 12:21 NIV

Father, I had planned to buy a pair of sneakers for outdoor walking. The sports store carried an array of choices—walking shoes, running shoes, rock-climbing shoes, cross-trainers, and sturdy hiking boots. Although I don't often think about my feet, the choices of footwear proved that they are as important as other parts of my body.

Lord, remind me that those who work for You are all part of the body of Christ. As a Christian, I am often unaware of the importance of people who work for You behind the scenes. They are hidden by their humility. Father, I pray that I will appreciate their efforts and tell them so. Guide me also to be a hidden servant.

Father, I want to instill in my children a respect for those who train them in the ways of righteousness. May my children recognize the selfless contributions of their teachers, coaches, sponsors, and other leaders, and show appreciation for their efforts.

# RENEWAL

*If we confess our sins, he is faithful and just and will forgive us our sins and purify us from all unrighteousness.*

1 JOHN 1:9 NIV

Father, I confess my sins and ask for pardon. I rejoice that You forgive my offenses. I am thankful that You are lenient with me and deal gently with me. You renew me each day so that I am free from the burden of sin. You lift me up so that I can begin each day refreshed in Your love. You help me recognize my shortcomings, but You give me the ability to go on despite them.

Lord, give me the strength to exercise patience with my children just as You exercise patience with me. I pray that I will forgive and encourage my children in such a way that they do not become dejected at their failures.

Father, I come to You with a submissive spirit and unquestioning faith in Your willingness to forgive me. I carry away from my prayer time a feeling of thanksgiving because my heart and mind are purified through You.

# OPEN MIND

*Train up a child in the way he should go:*
*and when he is old, he will not depart from it.*
PROVERBS 22:6 KJV

Father, my young son is at a wonderful age. Each morning I think about some new skill that I saw him display the previous day. Each night I delight in watching him throw himself into learning a new task. From climbing onto a chair, walking down stairs, tossing a ball, or stacking blocks, he attacks it with enthusiasm. I am both astonished and pleased at how fast the little one is developing.

Lord, I've seen birds in a nest open their mouths, ready to take whatever their parents deliver for them to eat. They fully trust their parents and never think that it might do them harm.

Father, it is a tremendous responsibility You have given me to raise my children. May I always be aware that their minds are as quick to absorb new information as their bodies are to learn new skills. Guide me as I put into their hearts the unwavering conviction that they can always trust You.

# FEARLESS

*But now, this is what the LORD says—he who created you,
O Jacob, he who formed you, O Israel: "Fear not, for I have
redeemed you; I have summoned you by name; you are mine."*

ISAIAH 43:1 NIV

Father, when I prayed for You to quell the doubts and fears
that troubled my mind, You helped me to overcome those
events that were in my power to change. You gave me the
emotional soundness to bear those trials that remained. I see now
that You put them there so that by enduring them I would gain
character and confidence.

Lord, You have given me experiences that improved my abilities
as a father. If I will be guided by You, ask for advice from Christians
who embrace Your wisdom, and pray to implement what I have
learned, then I will be able to be a father that my children can trust.

Heavenly Father, help me recognize
the distress of others when they
are in the valley. Let me support
them through their dark days.
Give me the wisdom to be an
encouragement to them. May I
learn to put my trust in You
and succeed in sharing that
trust with others.

# PROTECTION

*He is like a man which built an house, and digged deep,*
*and laid the foundation on a rock: and when the flood arose,*
*the stream beat vehemently upon that house, and could not shake it:*
*for it was founded upon a rock.*

LUKE 6:48 KJV

Dear Lord, as a young child, my walk home from a friend's house took me through a small patch of woods. This particular grove always appeared exceptionally dark. The moist earth around the roots carried an unpleasant dank smell. I would pull my coat around me and hurry through while I tried to act more brave than I actually felt.

Father, as my children grow older, the time comes for them to take small steps of their own into the world. Dangers, especially spiritual ones, are all around us. Please protect them in their journeys. I pray they put on Your robe of righteousness so Satan cannot harm them.

Jesus, I'm traveling through a realm where You have given Satan access. Although this world is not my final destination, I must pass through it while on my way home. I pray for You to cover me and surround me with Your atoning blood.

# DANGEROUSLY DEAD

*Trust ye in the LORD for ever:*
*for in the LORD JEHOVAH is everlasting strength.*

ISAIAH 26:4 KJV

Father, the great oak tree had become dangerously dead, but no one could tell. The death was in the heartwood, working from the inside out. When the storm came, the trunk snapped, fell, and crushed smaller trees nearby.

Lord, sometimes I have become captivated by people whom I considered towering Christians. But I could not see their hearts, and occasionally their lives collapsed because they had become but a shell of Christianity. When they fell, I became disillusioned. I pray that my trust will always be upon You as my ultimate, unfailing leader.

Father, I pray that my children understand that the only true role model for them is Jesus. It is easy for them to look up to adults who later prove to be less than worthy of their admiration. Guide me to help them understand that You are the only One who will never fail them.

# UNMASKED

*For the word of God is quick, and powerful,*
*and sharper than any twoedged sword, piercing even to the*
*dividing asunder of soul and spirit, and of the joints and marrow,*
*and is a discerner of the thoughts and intents of the heart.*

HEBREWS 4:12 KJV

Father, as a child I enjoyed putting on a disguise and pretending to be one of my heroes. The playacting did not end at childhood. As an adult, I modified my demeanor to match the situation. My choice of language, how I conducted myself, and the clothes I wore were selected to conform to what I imagined would help me fit in with my peers.

Father, I am always visible to You. May I develop the humble nature that can put off the disguise and instead work toward being the unique person You want me to be.

Lord, I have seen stress develop as the image a person tried to project differed too radically from his or her true self. Help my children understand that camouflaging themselves can become a charade that leads to stress, hollowness, and hypocrisy. Help them remain true to themselves and true to You.

# FINGERPRINTS

*For he saith to the snow, Be thou on the earth; likewise to the small rain,*
*and to the great rain of his strength. He sealeth up the hand*
*of every man; that all men may know his work.*

JOB 37:6–7 KJV

Father, we still have the prints made of our children's feet for identification after their birth. The tiny friction ridges identify them exactly. Although means of identification has advanced, such as DNA, the friction patterns on feet and fingers are still the preferred method of identification. A fingerprint cannot be changed or hidden. It makes each one of us unique.

O Lord, I pray that I treat each of my children as unique individuals, each with personal strengths and weaknesses. May I rejoice in their differences.

Father, fingerprinting brings to mind the many ways that You have signed Your likeness on the world—from snowflakes to the ridge patterns on my fingers. In our factories, mass production can make millions of things all identical, but You create billions of people, and no two are alike. I am a one-of-a-kind, special creation. Help me find and succeed at the unique role for which I am particularly qualified.

# GIFTS

*So we, being many, are one body in Christ,*
*and every one members one of another.*
*Having then gifts differing according. . .to the proportion of faith. . .*
ROMANS 12:5—6 KJV

Lord, as a child I would stand over an anthill and watch ants go about their business. I marveled at their ceaseless effort. Yet it bothered me that one worker ant was not clearly different from another.

Lord, I have worked to bring about in my children the understanding that they are Your special creation. My grandchildren are developing the same diversity. They are becoming more aware through their parents' teaching that they are unique because You have made them so.

Father, I rejoice that I have a unique personality. As a Christian, I have strengths and weaknesses. I have talents for some tasks but must depend upon others to carry out those jobs that I cannot do. I am Your gift to others—and they are Your gifts to me. Dear God, lead me as I use my individual abilities to share Your love with others.

# WRITE

*Do not let loyalty and faithfulness forsake you;*
*bind them around your neck, write them on the tablet of your heart.*
*So you will find favor and good repute in the sight of God and of people.*

PROVERBS 3:3−4 NRSV

Lord, with my Internet browser, I can specify the subjects that I want displayed when I log on. I can choose news content, weather reports, financial statements, sports scores, and entertainment guides. I can build a personal page that is unique to me.

Father, today You have given me a fresh page of my life. I can write upon it words that encourage or words that destroy, acts of kindness or selfish deeds, thoughts that cause my spirit to soar or ideas that bring me lower. Let me wisely choose the content of my life to glorify You.

Lord, I pray that my children will develop a sense of their purpose as a special creation of Yours. May they recognize that You have designed everyone to be special. Give them the insight to see how they can make a difference through their daily contact with others. Help them write the content of their life to You.

# CORNERSTONE

*"See, I am laying in Zion a stone, a cornerstone chosen and precious; and whoever believes in him will not be put to shame."*

1 PETER 2:6 NRSV

Heavenly Father, yesterday I helped as my little girl put together a puzzle. At first, the pieces were all mixed together without a pattern. It was confusing to her, and she didn't know where to start. I showed her one of the corner pieces. After she had that piece in place, one by one she succeeded in fitting the others together.

Lord, before I gave my heart to You and sought Your will, my life was a confusing collection of parts. But as I developed a personal relationship with You, a clearer image formed of what You have in store for me. I saw that putting my life back together became easier once I chose You as my starting point.

Although my daughter's future is not yet fully revealed, I pray that she will gladly put the disarrayed components of her life in Your hands to complete the picture.

# ROOTS

*But the fruit of the Spirit is love, joy, peace, longsuffering,*
*gentleness, goodness, faith, Meekness, temperance.*

GALATIANS 5:22–23 KJV

ather, weeds in my yard resisted my efforts to eradicate them.
Cutting them down at grass-top level did not destroy them.
They merely grew back. Stronger methods were needed,
such as digging the roots out by hand.

Lord, sometimes I have problems in my life that I treat too
lightly. I mask the symptoms at the surface level without looking for
the cause that goes deeper. The problems reappear because I have
not attacked the root of them. Help me find lasting answers to those
things that should not be in my life.

Father, let me recognize in myself and in my children those
habits that allow sin to take root. Rescue us and help us weed out by
the roots rebellion, apathy, resentment, and
destructive tendencies. Help us
be effective in replacing them
with love, joy, peace, patience,
and all the fruit of the Holy
Sprit.

# PREVAIL

*For the love of God is this, that we obey his commandments.*
*And his commandments are not burdensome,*
*for whatever is born of God conquers the world.*
*And this is the victory that conquers the world, our faith.*

1 JOHN 5:3–4 NRSV

Father, I often take too long to weigh the pros and cons of a situation. Help me quickly recognize and eliminate those choices that are outside the Christian realm. I want to overcome the evil in my life.

I can only be defeated because I am inconsistent in my dedication to You. I hesitate when I should press the attack. Give me the determination to serve only You and the faith to stand firmly on the side of righteousness.

Lord, through my lack of perseverance, my children can become the innocent victims of heartless evil. Protect them when my protection grows weak. Father, I want to master the adversary and bring my evil desires into submission. Give me the strength to prevail whether it is a swift victory or a prolonged battle. May I never view success as the end of the struggle, but instead remain vigilant to the ongoing efforts of Satan to thwart Your plan for my life.

# SERVICE

*I can do all things through Christ which strengtheneth me.*

PHILIPPIANS 4:13 KJV

Father, I go out each day as a soldier for You. If I am rewarded with victory after victory, may I examine my goals in case I am aiming too low. Teach me to see clearly the battles You want me to fight. Give me the ability to think the impossible, and fill me with the aggressive faith to make it happen.

Lord, may I never use my understanding of Your commands to launch a personal attack on individuals. I want to firmly stand for what is right and do so in such a way that Your love dominates the situation. Help me instill in my children the understanding that we must follow Your will despite what others might be doing.

Father, battles are long and victories are short. I would rather enjoy victories than failure, but I would rather suffer a lost battle than stand on the sidelines doing nothing. Almighty God, I surrender myself to Your service.

# RESIST

*Submit yourselves therefore to God. Resist the devil,*
*and he will flee from you.*

JAMES 4:7 KJV

Lord, my visits to the zoo with my children always include a tour through the reptile house. The boa constrictor is big and strong. The poisonous rattlesnake imparts fear by the warning rattle of its tail. At first, the snakes repelled my children, but as their fear diminished, they became fascinated by them. They put their faces close to the glass to see every detail.

Father, a walk by the snakes reminds me of the analogy of Satan to a serpent. I explain to my children that unlike reptiles that avoid humans and strike only because they feel danger is near, Satan hunts victims to attack. I reminded them that sin could also lure them closer. At first sin repels them, but should they grow accustomed to it, they could be easily enticed to participate in it.

Protective Lord, thank You for the promise that we can have victory over Satan by resisting him through Your name.

# ROAD MAP

*I will lead the blind by ways they have not known,*
*along unfamiliar paths I will guide them; I will turn the darkness*
*into light before them and make the rough places smooth.*
*These are the things I will do; I will not forsake them.*

ISAIAH 42:16 NIV

Lord, I plan a driving trip in exhaustive detail, highlighting the best route on the map, pinning down stopovers, and identifying points of interest. All of this requires a great deal of study that begins weeks before the departure date. Shortly before we leave, I check the car's oil and other fluids and the air pressure in the tires. After we pack and are ready to go, I make sure the baby is in his car seat and everyone is securely buckled. I do not want anything to go wrong.

Father, I pray that I take even more care in planning my heavenly trip. I don't know how much time I have to prepare for it, but while there is still time, I will talk to You in prayer, study the Bible to learn Your will, and work to be a faithful servant. I pray that my concern to secure my children's physical safety is only exceeded by my efforts for their spiritual well-being.

## PLEASING PATTERNS

*Whatever you have learned or received or heard from me,*
*or seen in me—put it into practice.*
*And the God of peace will be with you.*

PHILIPPIANS 4:9 NIV

Father, frequent repetition causes me to acquire a behavior that becomes an unconscious habit. When I fall into a habit and allow my conscious mind to give up its responsibilities, I glide through the activity without really thinking.

Lord, it seems the habits that I pick up most readily are the bad ones. In Your Word, I read to guard against bad habits such as failing to meet with other Christians and being idle. I mistrust a habit because it is an action without thinking. So I pray that I am always mindful of what I am doing. Only then can I assess whether I am following Your will and making the right choices. I want to develop acceptable practices and help my children do the same.

Help me, Father, exchange these old eyes for new ones. Let me look at my life and recognize unconscious habits, especially the bad ones. Help me change them into a conscious pattern pleasing to You.

# COBWEBS

*He lies in wait near the villages;*
*from ambush he murders the innocent,*
*watching in secret for his victims.*

PSALM 10:8 NIV

Heavenly Father, spiders spin webs to snare wandering insects. They are found in most locations worldwide. I have seen spider webs in obscure places, and I wonder why an insect would ever be trapped. But the spider knows how to capture unsuspecting victims.

Father, I know that Satan, too, catches valuable souls in a web of sin. Often the temptation is placed in an unsuspecting location. Like spiders, he spins his web of deceit worldwide. His influence can be found in all places.

Lord, guard my mind, body, and spirit from Satan's lures. Deliver me from the temptation to violate Your laws. Only with Your help can I maintain a holy lifestyle and avoid becoming a victim seized by deception. My children are appealing targets for the forces of destruction. Protect them against the lure of Satan that would wrap them in the sticky web of sin.

# LIFETIME LOVE

*Each of you, however, should love his wife as himself,*
*and a wife should respect her husband.*

EPHESIANS 5:33 NRSV

L ord, I've heard that a husband prays for You to keep his wife the sweet person he married, and a wife prays for You to change her husband into the man she wants him to be. Instead, I will pray that You make us what *You* want us to be.

Father, I ask You to strengthen my wife in the many tasks that are part of being a mother to our children. I pray that we work together to make the right decisions in raising them. Looking ahead, may we always keep in mind that after they have left home, our love for one another will not have diminished but instead will have grown richer from the experience.

I am thankful, Lord, that I married the woman I loved, and today I can say I love the woman I married. I pray that I will respect her as a faithful partner, and we will walk side by side in the path You direct.

# Captivated

*May your fountain be blessed, and may you rejoice in the wife of your youth. A loving doe, a graceful deer—may her breasts satisfy you always, may you ever be captivated by her love.*

Proverbs 5:18–19 NIV

Father, thank You for revealing the loveliness of my wife to me. I can see You in her actions. At the end of a trying day, she still shows sweet patience with our children. She consoles an upset child as if his ache were all that mattered. She makes pain go away merely by her soothing kiss. She does the same for me. She sees bravery, strength, and ability when I see none of those heroic qualities. She is the most beautiful person in my life.

Lord, for some people, love is a thunderstorm—intense but of short duration. Encourage our enthusiasm for one another so that it endures. I pray that our love is everlasting, earnest, and selfless.

Father, I want to care for my wife, embrace her, and cherish her. May I continue to develop a oneness with her that I share with no other person. I pray that we create a future where we act in agreement with our shared hopes and dreams.

# BOND

*Therefore a man leaves his father and his mother*
*and clings to his wife, and they become one flesh.*

GENESIS 2:24 NRSV

Father, I pray that my wife and I will show one another the love You have shown to us. May we be bound together in affection—two minds with but a single mission. When we work together toward spiritual goals, we feel our love for one another and for You stronger than on any other occasion. May we complement and complete one another so our separate, personal goals combine to become a single effort to serve You.

Lord, our victories have not all been won, but together we press ahead. We have so much in common—a common love for You and for our children and a determination to live lives worthy of one another's respect. Father, I am confident that my wife and I are dedicated to bringing our lives into alignment with Your will. May we speak often with You, study Your Word, live in Your assurance, and pursue Your righteousness.

# HARMONY

*May the God of steadfastness and encouragement grant you
to live in harmony with one another, in accordance with Christ Jesus,
so that together you may with one voice glorify the God
and Father of our Lord Jesus Christ.*

ROMANS 15:5−6 NRSV

Father, I want for my wife and me to live in the union of Your love. Help us develop the trust to share with one another all of our fears, hopes, and dreams. May we always rejoice in one another's victories and mitigate one another's failures. Guide us to work together to overcome problems that our marriage may encounter.

Lord, my wife is a delight to me. When I experience sorrow, she shares the sadness but draws me out to joy. When I am dejected, she makes me cheerful. She fills my heart with optimism.

Father, grant me the sensitivity to recognize when discord and distance begin to separate us. I pray that I'll never let a moment of reckless folly drive a wedge of sin between us. I put myself under Your control and sacrifice my personal motives to bring harmony to my marriage.

# ABOUT THE AUTHOR

JOHN HUDSON TINER is the author of high-interest-level Bible study and devotion books. He has more than seventy books published, and his material has been translated into a variety of languages. Tiner, who gave his heart to Jesus at an early age, is well known for his books about the interaction of science and religion. He also compiled the Barbour book *Show Me Your Love*, a collection of 366 daily devotions on love by classical Christian writers. He and his wife, D. Jeanene Tiner, a photographer, have been married for forty-three years, and they have two children and six grandchildren.

# SCRIPTURE INDEX